# EDINBU

## The Dorothy Dunnett Guide

Nicky Cannon

THE DOROTHY DUNNETT SOCIETY
Edinburgh
Scottish Charity No. SC030649
dorothydunnett.org

In memory of Dorothy Dunnett, who gave so much pleasure to so many.

*There is no land uninhabitable or sea unnavigable.*
*(*The Ringed Castle, *part 3, chapter 9)*

# Contents

| | |
|---|---|
| *Maps* | *iv* |
| **Introduction** | 1 |
| Edinburgh in the Landscape | 3 |
| Growth of the Capital City | 5 |
| Edinburgh – A Fortified City | 7 |
| The Backbone of Edinburgh | 11 |
| **Locations** | 14 |
| A  The Castle | 14 |
| B  Below the Castle | 20 |
| C  Castlehill and Lawnmarket | 24 |
|     The High Street | 30 |
| D  Upper High Street – South Side | 31 |
| E  Upper High Street – North Side | 43 |
| F  Lower High Street | 46 |
| G  Canongate | 50 |
| H  Holyrood | 56 |
| **Excursions** | 60 |
| Craigmillar Castle | 60 |
| Leith | 63 |
| Musselburgh | 66 |
| Roslin/Rosslyn | 67 |
| **Places of Interest** | 71 |
| *Map in two parts: 'A Bird's-Eye View of Edinburgh in 1647' by James Gordon of Rothiemay* | 74 |
| *Glossary* | 78 |
| *Index* | 79 |
| *Publishing Information and Credits* | 84 |

**MAPS**

| | | |
|---|---|---|
| | Edinburgh, Canongate and the Surrounding Villages in the 16th Century | 4 |
| | Edinburgh's Defensive Walls | 9 |
| | The Old Town | 12–13 |
| A | Edinburgh Castle | 15 |
| B | Below the Castle | 21 |
| C | Castlehill and Lawnmarket | 25 |
| D | Upper High Street – South Side | 31 |
| | The High Kirk of St Giles | 33 |
| E | Upper High Street – North Side | 43 |
| F | Lower High Street | 47 |
| G | Canongate | 52–53 |
| H | Holyrood | 57 |
| I | Craigmillar Castle | 60 |
| J | The National Museum of Scotland | 71 |

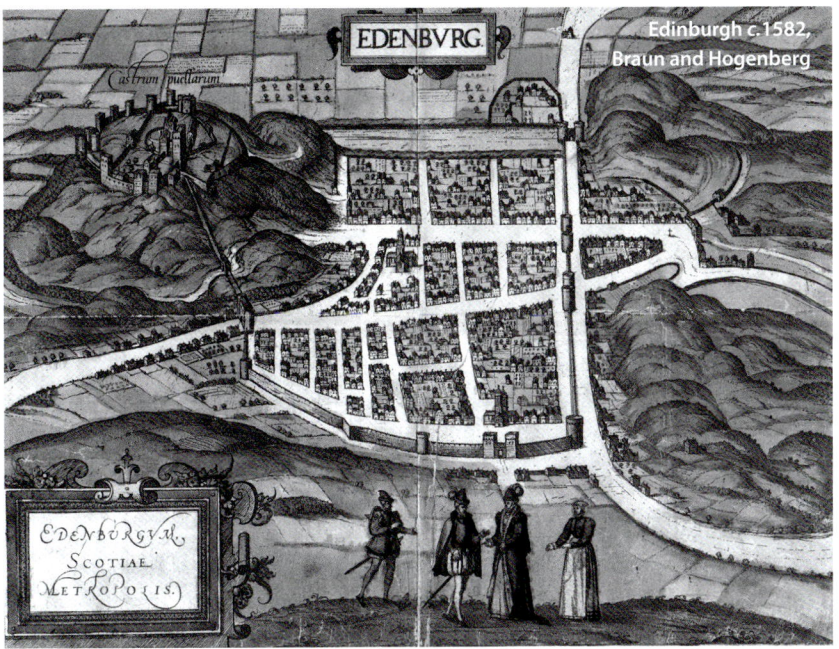

Edinburgh c.1582, Braun and Hogenberg

# Introduction

This is a guide to the Edinburgh of Dorothy Dunnett's historical novels. It is not intended to be a comprehensive guide to this beautiful city. A commercial travel guide and a good map are absolutely necessary to enjoy Edinburgh to the full.

It is designed to remind you of the Dorothy Dunnett connections in Edinburgh and will draw your attention to the whereabouts of features that appear in the books but no longer exist. Hopefully, it will also be useful to readers who are unable to visit Edinburgh but who would like to visualise locations and key events. Quotations from the books have been included to remind you of what happened, where and to whom.

Nicholas vander Poele, the central character in The House of Niccolò series, comes to Edinburgh when he first arrives in Scotland in 1468 in *The Unicorn Hunt* (*UH*). The city also features in *To Lie With Lions* (*TLWL*) and *Gemini* (*Gem*). It is already the capital of Scotland: the residence of the court and the country's political and legal centre. Its growing population and expanding mercantile interests mean that Nicholas is an incredibly good fit with the Edinburgh of the time. Already wealthy, his bank and trading connections allow him to enter society at a high level of influence with the court and the merchant burgesses of Edinburgh.

The hero of The Lymond Chronicles, Francis Crawford of Lymond's first appearance is his stealthy entrance to Edinburgh in the opening scene of *The Game of Kings* (*GoK*) in 1547. The High Street is the setting for the climactic final scenes of *The Disorderly Knights* (*DK*) and Lymond passes through in *The Ringed Castle* (*RC*) with the Russian delegation. The Culters have a house there, as do the Scotts, but Lymond's relationship with Edinburgh is different from that of Nicholas for, although it is there that he conducts some business, is brought to trial and faces Gabriel, he does not live there. Edinburgh is important to the Stuart monarchy, and therefore to Scotland, so Lymond is drawn back there repeatedly when he is in the country.

In *King Hereafter* (*KH*), Edinburgh, known by its older name Dunedin, lies within Lothian, which is a source of repeated dispute between Thorfinn and Earl Siward over lands and income.

Edinburgh is where Dorothy Dunnett made her home for many years, and all her books were written there. She wrote, therefore, having experienced the city in all its moods and seasons, and with considerable affection.

Dorothy Dunnett's description of the town is often detailed but is also, at times, carefully vague. Edinburgh Castle, the great church of St Giles and the Palace of Holyroodhouse are easily recognisable even if they are much changed since the times of the books. Some buildings and streets no longer exist but their sites can be accurately pinpointed, and there are only hints of the whereabouts of some characters' homes. On occasion, we have to remember that in fiction, settings and buildings can sometimes be fictional too.

Sometimes this guide will point to features that do not appear in the books but which serve as exemplars of those that characters might have seen or known. The one relevant museum situated on the Royal Mile is noted in the appropriate place in the sequence. Others, with notes about artefacts of interest, are grouped together under 'Places of Interest'.

The guide begins with an outline of the geographical and historical background of the city and is then divided into sections directly related to the text of the novels.

**Locations:** The Edinburgh of the novels is mostly confined to the Old Town, that part of the city comprising the original burghs of Edinburgh and Canongate. The locations are therefore restricted to the street now known as the Royal Mile and the area immediately surrounding it. The Royal Mile runs downhill west to east from the Castle to Holyrood, but this official collective name was not invented until the late 19th century and even now is not always used by locals. Individual sections (from west to east) are Castle Esplanade, Castlehill, Lawnmarket, High Street, Canongate and Abbey Strand. 'High Street' is still in common usage as a way of describing all the parts of the road in the old burgh of Edinburgh.

Closes run down the slopes on either side of the High Street: south to the Grassmarket and the Cowgate and north to Princes Street Gardens (once the Nor' Loch). South Bridge and George IV Bridge, built in the 19th century, now span the hollow to the south with the Cowgate running beneath, whilst North Bridge spans the hollow to the north and runs above Waverley Station. Bank Street and the Mound descend the northern slope opposite George IV Bridge, crossing the hollow and the site of the Nor' Loch next to the National Gallery of Scotland.

Some of the numbered locations are now overlaid by new geography or buildings and they appear with the modern location named first and the name from the books following in brackets, where they are different. Hopefully, it is clear when the readers are being asked to join Dorothy Dunnett in conjuring features from their imaginations.

The death of Buccleuch, and the fight in St Giles' *(DK*, Pt 3, Ch 17*)* are both outlined, as is the Nativity Play *(TLWL*, Pt 2, Ch 17 and 18*)* so that the reader can follow the course of the action in those climactic scenes.

**Excursions:** Craigmillar Castle, Leith, Musselburgh (site of the Battle of Pinkie), Rosslyn Chapel and Castle and their relevance to the books are described. 'The Affair of the Poisoned Soup' (*Gem*, Ch 17 and 18) is detailed in this section.

**Places of Interest:** This section details other locations that are of interest to the Dunnett reader. The National Gallery of Scotland, the Scottish National Portrait Gallery, the National Museum of Scotland and the National Library of Scotland all have items that are relevant to the books.

**The Rothiemay Map of 1647:** The pictorial 'Bird's-Eye View of Edinburgh' drawn by James Gordon (1615–86) clearly shows the distinct features of the city, many of which are described in this guide.

## Edinburgh in the Landscape

The capital of Scotland, Edinburgh lies on the southern shoreline of the Firth of Forth, a river estuary in the eastern lowlands. The modern city encompasses the port of Leith, its original link to the sea, and the villages that grew up on the small hills nearby, having expanded far beyond the original settlement. The Pentland Hills rise from the south-west outskirts of the modern city and run in an unbroken line nearly to Biggar, Boghall and Midculter. To the south-east lies the vale of the River Tyne and beyond that the eastern hills of the Southern Uplands.

In *King Hereafter*, Thorfinn looks over towards Lothian in the distance from the hill of Dumyat, near Stirling, as he anticipates battle:

> *Below them, from right to left, the river Forth ran to the sea: a silver inlay of zigzags in a great plain chequered with corn and green mosses, and the harsh buff and sliced resilient brown of peat beds. Beyond the river, the plain married into wandering uplands ... to end far to the left, where sea and sky met, with the crag, small and clear, of Dunedin.* (KH, Pt 4, Ch 5)

Edinburgh and Canongate grew up less than 3 miles from the sea, on a crag and tail formation left 10,000 years ago by the last Ice Age. The Castle Rock is the basalt plug of a long extinct volcano, which rises with sheer sides some 134 metres above sea level. The tail forms a ridge sloping down from the heights of the Castle. Edinburgh grew eastwards down this ridge and, later, Canongate grew westward up from Holyrood. The two burghs eventually developed to meet where the wall of Edinburgh crossed the thoroughfare at a highly fortified gate called the Netherbow. The city at that time was surrounded by hills, many of which it has now encompassed. Calton Hill rises up from the city on the way to Leith, and Arthur's Seat and Salisbury Crags lie by Holyrood.

Dorothy Dunnett gives a sense of how Edinburgh sat in its landscape in several pieces

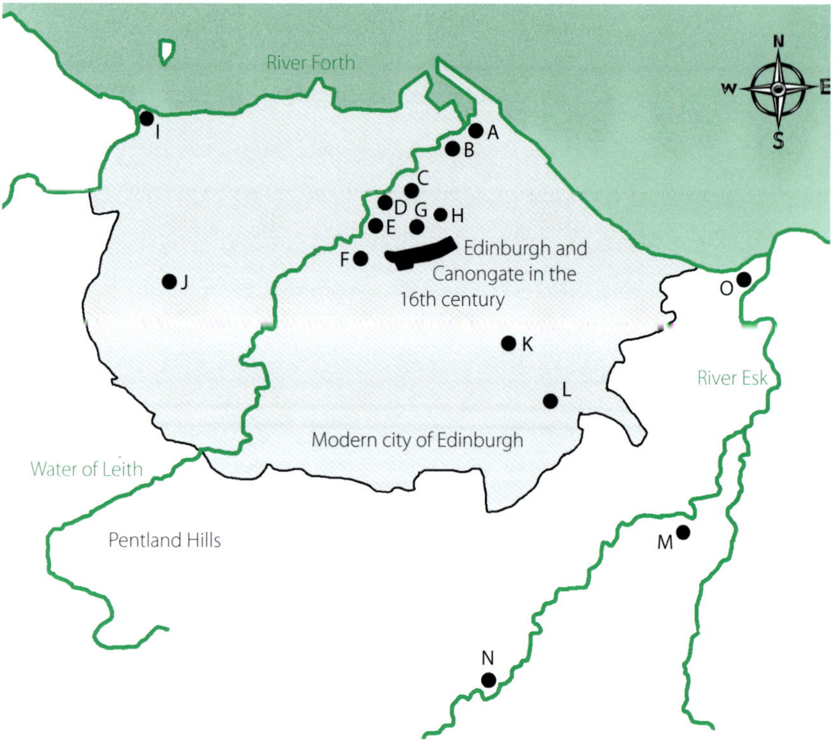

**EDINBURGH, CANONGATE AND THE SURROUNDING VILLAGES IN THE 16TH CENTURY**

| | | | | | |
|---|---|---|---|---|---|
| A | Leith | F | Kirkbraehead | K | Craigmillar |
| B | Bonnington | G | Moultrie's Hill | L | Edmonstone |
| C | Broughton | H | Greenside | M | Dalkeith |
| D | Canonmills | I | Cramond | N | Roslin |
| E | Silvermills | J | Costorphine | O | Musselburgh |

of beautifully wrought prose. When Lymond and Nepeja arrive from the north after the shipwreck:

> *Separated ... from his mentor and able, at last, to unbutton his normal thought processes, Osep Nepeja's first words on standing on the hill of Corstorphine and beholding, far over the marsh, the end-rock and castle of Edinburgh, bore witness to a long and weary journey, of which this was by no means the end. 'Do we climb it on ropes?' he remarked. 'Or do they take up the horses in buckets?'* (RC, Pt 3, Ch 4)

Corstorphine is one of the villages that are now part of the modern city and from the characters' perspective, looking east, only the Castle was visible. Nicholas, on the other hand, looks out from the castle towards the north where Fife lies beyond the River Forth:

*His gaze ... rested on the darkness beneath the outer wall of the Castle, and the silent glimmering mass of the town plunging beyond, with the black pool of the Nor' Loch below it. And far beyond that, over dark country ridges and the faint lights of towers and townships, was the broad grey span of the estuary and the black hills of Fife brooding behind.* (TLWL, Pt 2, Ch 12)

## Growth of the Capital City

Settlement in the area dates back to well before historical records, although little of these early residents remains in archaeological evidence, with the earliest data from the Bronze Age around 9,000 BC. The site of Edinburgh with its defensible rock dominating a fertile landscape and easy access to the sea must have been attractive to these early people. The Romans recognised it as a significant area and reported a hill fort on Castle Rock. Although they did not add to this, they did build other defences such as those at Cramond, once a coastal village and now part of modern Edinburgh. The defensibility of the crag has been both curse and blessing for Edinburgh as it has been an almost irresistible prize for those who have wished to control the lands beyond. So it proved in the 7th century for the Northumbrians, who defeated the native Goddodin and drove them from their stronghold of Din Eydin. These invaders from the south brought their culture and language to this part of Scotland, which had an impact in the ensuing centuries.

In the 11th century, the time of *King Hereafter*, the lands of Lothian and, at its centre, Dunedin were disputed, negotiated and fought over by the leaders of the emerging kingdom of Scotland and her interested neighbours. Thorfinn receives a report of Earl Siward and the Northumbrian army's advance:

*'They are between the hills and the Forth and are sparing nothing in Lothian, from the east coast to Dunedin. They are making no haste, and suffering no losses that matter. But for its refugees, Lothian and its southlands are dead.'* (KH, Pt 4, Ch 5)

In the 12th century, David I, probably influenced by time spent in England, modernised the administration of Scotland by creating autonomous administrative centres called 'burghs'. Edinburgh was one of the four original royal burghs of Scotland, and by degrees the most important and the wealthiest. It developed a monopoly on international trade and on the buying and selling of certain goods, with taxes paid in coin directly to the monarchy. Jurisdiction over Leith was granted to Edinburgh by Robert I's charter in 1329, and enhanced foreign trade. Ecclesiastical power, administration, law and wealth followed. Although the royal court was initially peripatetic, the kings of Scotland increasingly returned to Edinburgh as the seat of power, and it gradually assumed the status of the capital of Scotland during the 15th century.

## St Giles'

As Edinburgh grew in status, so did her parish church. The church of St Giles has stood in the High Street, down the ridge from the Castle, through Reformation, decay and refurbishment, and although not entirely the same as the one that stood in the 15th and 16th centuries, much remains.

St Giles was an Athenian hermit and healer, who settled in the south of France in

Interior of St Giles'

around the 7th century, and cured a sick beggar by giving him his cloak. He lived in the forest of Nîmes with a tame hind as his only companion. A hunter shot at the hind and wounded Giles, who refused personal riches as compensation, using the money to found a monastery instead. St Giles is typically depicted with a hind, protecting it from an arrow with his own body. He is the patron saint of lepers, the lame, blacksmiths and nursing mothers.

The earliest record of a parish church in Edinburgh dates back to 854 and the first stone church on this site was founded by David I around 1124. The first dedication ceremony by the Bishop of St Andrews was in 1243. A few carvings embedded into the fabric of the later church are all that remains of David I's Norman building, although the north door, highly decorated with faces, animals and geometric patterns, survived until the 18th century.

The building seems to have been extensively damaged by Edward II's English army in the early 14th century as there are records of building work after the army raided Edinburgh. The larger, 14th-century church was planned around the four octagonal pillars at the crossing, which are made of quartz-rich sandstone. Although this building was also damaged at the hands of the English, it was not destroyed. Improved and extended over the centuries, the current church is built in the Gothic style of the 15th century, with 19th-century restoration and additions.

In the 1450s Sir William Preston acquired a sacred relic of St Giles, which he donated to the church. He travelled to France and successfully negotiated with Charles VII for an arm bone. The relic was kept at the high altar in a gold reliquary in the shape of an arm and hand with a diamond on the finger, but was destroyed during the Reformation.

Following James III's application to the Vatican, St Giles' was granted Collegiate Church status in 1467. The king showed considerable devotion to St Giles', funding yearly requiem masses there for his father, and donating considerable sums of money. Some of this money was dowry from Princess Cicely of England, even though the contracted marriage to James III's son did not take place. This is important in the Anglo-Scottish conflict that takes place in *Gemini*. The crown spire, one of the distinctive points on the Edinburgh skyline, was added in 1500. At the end of James IV's reign in 1513 the bell of St Giles' tolled, summoning the citizens to defend the city after the catastrophic defeat at Flodden.

### Canongate – Edinburgh's Neighbour

The neighbouring burgh of the Canongate takes its name from the Augustinian Canons of the Abbey of Holyrood. The Abbey was founded in 1128 when David I granted land to the order at the eastern end of the ridge. Legend tells that the king, whilst hunting, had a vision of a stag with a cross between its antlers that guided him to build the new church. The arms of the Canongate still bear a white hart's head, a cross between its horns, and the motto *Sic itur ad Astra* ('Thus you shall go to the stars', from Virgil's *Aeneid*). It was dedicated to the Holy Rood, which may have been associated with a relic of the True Cross brought to Scotland by David's mother, St Margaret.

David also gave permission for the monks to establish a new burgh that was granted regality status giving it jurisdiction over the area now known as the Pleasance, part of the port of Leith and of the village of Broughton. The Abbey was enlarged during major works, which lasted until 1230, with the addition of monastic buildings including guest houses. It became a highly prestigious religious house; the Abbey had long had an association with royalty and accommodated several meetings of the Scottish Parliament in the 13th and 14th centuries. The vault of the church continued to need work over the years and flying buttresses were added in the 15th century to support the roof.

The Palace at Holyrood grew out of the royal habit of using rooms at the Abbey during the 15th and 16th centuries. By the later 15th century the royal court had established a permanent claim to part of the guest quarters, and James IV built the first Palace of Holyroodhouse adjoining the Abbey. During the Rough Wooing, when England was trying to abduct the child Mary, Queen of Scots, both Abbey and Palace were badly damaged by the English army under Lord Hertford, the Duke of Somerset, in 1544 and 1547.

Settlement in the Canongate originally sprang up near the Abbey and then spread up the hill towards the Netherbow. In the 15th and 16th centuries it became a desirable and prosperous place to live, independent yet linked to the structures of Edinburgh.

# Edinburgh – A Fortified City
## The Castle
For many centuries Edinburgh derived military and defensive power from the steep crag of Castle Rock, the longest continuously fortified place in the British Isles. This provided a precipitous defensible bastion that was an ample deterrent to the invader who was tempted by the wealth of Edinburgh. The early town sheltered along the highest part of the ridge and was originally protected by an area of marshland in the hollow to the north.

By the 12th century Edinburgh Castle was known in chronicles and in royal charters as 'Maiden Castle' or 'Castellum Puerellum' and the name remained in some usage until the 16th century. It is not clear why this name became attached, although theories abound including a place of safety for Pictish noblewomen, the location of a nunnery or links to Arthurian legend. It became the chief royal stronghold during the early medieval period, holding significant strategic importance.

As Scotland became a nation, Edinburgh, with its natural defences and rich trade routes, became steadily more important to the early kings. The oldest building remains St Margaret's Chapel but the Castle has been remodelled over the ages having been subject to siege, violence and military necessity. Much of the early Castle, possibly of Norman design, was destroyed in 1314 on the orders of Robert the Bruce during the Wars of Independence to make it unusable by English forces. Robert's son, David II, oversaw its reconstruction, including the building of David's Tower, which was completed some

Edinburgh Castle

years after his death in 1371. The smaller Constable's Tower was built at approximately the same time and from then on entrance to the Castle was through this round tower until the Lang Siege (1571–73).

As well as a fortress, the Castle was a royal residence, even if its highly defensible position did expose its inhabitants to the full force of the elements. During James IV's reign there was an increasing move towards using the more comfortable and gently situated Holyrood as a residence, although the Castle was still used when more security was required.

David's Tower was destroyed by cannon fire in the period after Mary, Queen of Scots was forced to abdicate in 1567 in favour of her infant son. Even after Mary had left Scotland, she still inspired loyalty amongst her supporters, who held Edinburgh Castle against the regency forces during the Lang Seige. When asked for aid by the Protestant pro-regency besiegers, Elizabeth of England sent heavy guns, which succeeded in badly damaging the Castle and forcing the occupying troops to surrender. Thereafter the Castle was used as a garrison, a military prison and finally an historic monument that forms the backdrop to several annual events, such as the Military Tattoo, Hogmanay celebrations and the Edinburgh Festival Fireworks Concert. It is the regimental headquarters of the Royal Regiment of Scotland.

More details about the Castle are given in Locations, below.

### Walls

Edinburgh's first wall was likely associated with the founding of the royal burgh in the 12th century but there is now little evidence for its construction. There is a reference to defences between the burghs of Edinburgh and Canongate in 1330; however, the first fully documented wall was built in the 15th century. In 1450 James II granted a licence for the building of the King's Wall to protect the settlement growing along and down

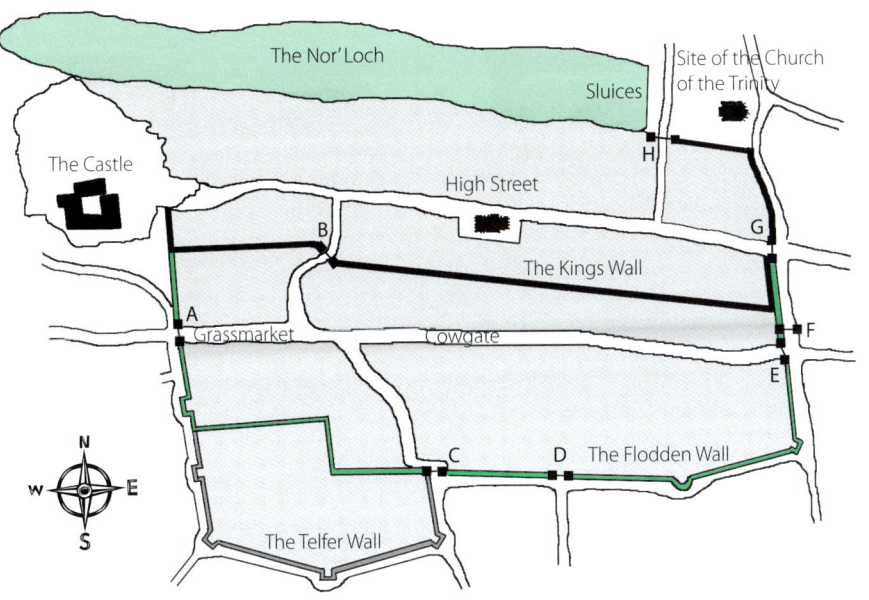

**EDINBURGH'S DEFENSIVE WALLS**

A   West Port
B   West or Upper Bow
C   Bristo Port
D   Potterow or Kirk o' Field Port
E   Cowgate Port
F   St Mary's Port
G   The Netherbow
H   New Port

the sides of the ridge against *oure enemies of England*, although it took at least 20 years to be completed. It ran eastward from the Castle and bounded the city parallel to the High Street, halfway down the hill towards the Cowgate. It turned north to divide the burgh of Edinburgh from that of the Canongate, then ran down the northern slope to the marsh.

By the time of the Scottish defeat at Flodden in 1513, Edinburgh had extended beyond the existing walls. Residential areas in the Cowgate and Grassmarket, and priories at Blackfriars, Kirk o' Field and Greyfriars were outwith the protection of the city wall. Also, the new threat of invasion from England had become more of a concern and magistrates decided to build a new wall to protect more of the city. The Flodden Wall ran south, down the Castle Rock from David's Tower across the hollow containing the Grassmarket and up the opposite slope. It turned east to run parallel to and south of the Cowgate, encompassing the religious houses, and then turned north to meet with the King's Wall near the Netherbow. This huge project was expensive and parts were still under construction by the end of The Lymond Chronicles but, even so, the new walls meant that Lymond has to swim the Nor' Loch to get into the city in *The Game of Kings*:

> ... *the total defeat by England thirty-four years since at Flodden had caused high walls to be flung around Edinburgh which were damnably inopportune ... for*

*Crawford of Lymond, now parting the flat waters of the Nor' Loch like an oriflamme in the wake of the boat.* (GoK, Opening Gambit)

The Telfer Wall was built in the 17th century as an extension that encompassed more land south of the Castle. Older city walls still defended buildings and closes, although most decayed or were demolished in the ensuing centuries. Also, lands and houses continued to have their own walls and in places they contributed to the defences of Edinburgh. Closes were also often defensible in their own right.

The city gates were known as 'ports' from the French or as 'bows' to reflect their arched shape. Many of these are mentioned in Dorothy Dunnett's books, and although none now remain, some are remembered in the surrounding street names or marked on pavements. The King's Wall had only two principal gates, the Netherbow and the West or Upper Bow; the Flodden Wall had six. Reference to the gates mentioned in the books is made in the relevant Locations, below.

## The Nor' Loch

In 1460 James III ordered the creation of a lake by building a dam at the eastern end of the boggy ground north of the Castle, in order to improve the defences north of the town. The result was the Nor' Loch (North Loch), a lake that measured about 800 x 125 metres and stretched from the base of Castle Rock to where the east city wall ran down from the Netherbow, near the eastern end of what is now Waverley Station.

The loch would sometimes freeze over as it does in *To Lie With Lions*, providing an impromptu skating rink.

> *All the rest of the year, the Nor' Loch lay in its hollow below the steep ridge of the High Street and mirrored the Castle in its flat reedy expanse. Turned to ice, it now reflected the red of the sunset ...* (TLWL, Pt 4, Ch 41)

The dam and sluices were at the eastern end.

> *[Mistress Clémence said] 'this is an artificial lake only thirty years old, created to defend the north side of the Castle. It is fed from the well-house over there, and by springs. Its height is controlled by a dam and sluice at the east end, by the Trinity College gardens, through which the sluice water runs. Skating is perfectly safe so long as the water is frozen quite solid, but care is required as the season advances ... if you lay your ear to the ice, you will hear a murmur of fresh running water. It is not frozen solid.'* (TLWL, Pt 4, Ch 41)

Lymond swims the Nor' Loch to enter the city covertly via Mungo Tennant's cellar.

> *Among the reeds of the Nor' Loch, where the snipe and the woodcock lay close and the baillies' swans raised their grey necks, a man quietly stripped to silk shirt and hose and stood listening, before sliding softly into the water.* (GoK, Opening Gambit)

Waste and rubbish drained into the Nor' Loch, particularly from the closes on the north side of the Royal Mile, and this became an increasing public health problem over time. It was also used as a place for the trial by *douking* (ducking) of witches, and when it was drained a number of human remains were found. The Nor' Loch was drained in stages over the 18th and 19th centuries as part of the expansion and improvement of the city. Princes Street Gardens, running between Old and New Towns and opened as a public park in 1820, now lies in its stead.

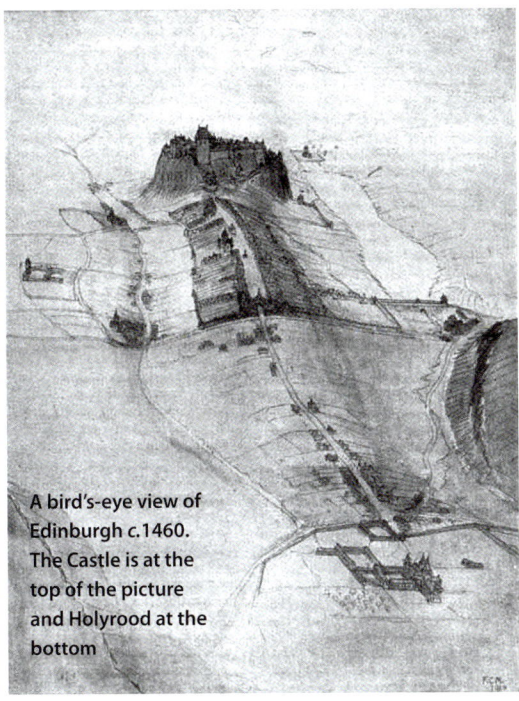

A bird's-eye view of Edinburgh c.1460. The Castle is at the top of the picture and Holyrood at the bottom

## The Backbone of Edinburgh
### Closes

The Royal Mile has been likened to the spine of a fish with its ribs the passageways that run down the slopes from the ridge. These are known generically as closes, but may have other names such as entry, court, vennel and wynd. In this quote, Dorothy Dunnett calls them pends:

> *They were given a house in the High Street, the steep cobbled main street of Edinburgh ... Nepeja saw a thoroughfare lined with tall grey stone houses, each with its turnpike stair; its flight of steps from first floor to street. And since, shoulder to shoulder, they admitted no entrance between them, you found your way through them by pends, arched tunnels pierced in the stonework which led through to green sloping gardens, their limits washed by a broad lake. (RC, Pt 3, Ch 4)*

Closes led between the buildings, called lands, which themselves were built upon strips of ground known as tofts. Once individual properties with houses at street level, these lands extended down from the ridge to gardens and smallholdings. A house therefore could be located both on a close and on the main street. For example, the Culter house lies on the High Street and Bruce's Close. Closes were often named after a significant resident.

As the population grew, the open ground began to be filled by more dwellings and people crowded together in the closes, in buildings that extended from a more modest height in Nicholas's day to more than twelve storeys by the 17th century. Status and wealth influenced at which floor level an individual lived. The rich tended to live on the first and second floors and the houses directly situated on the main thoroughfare were

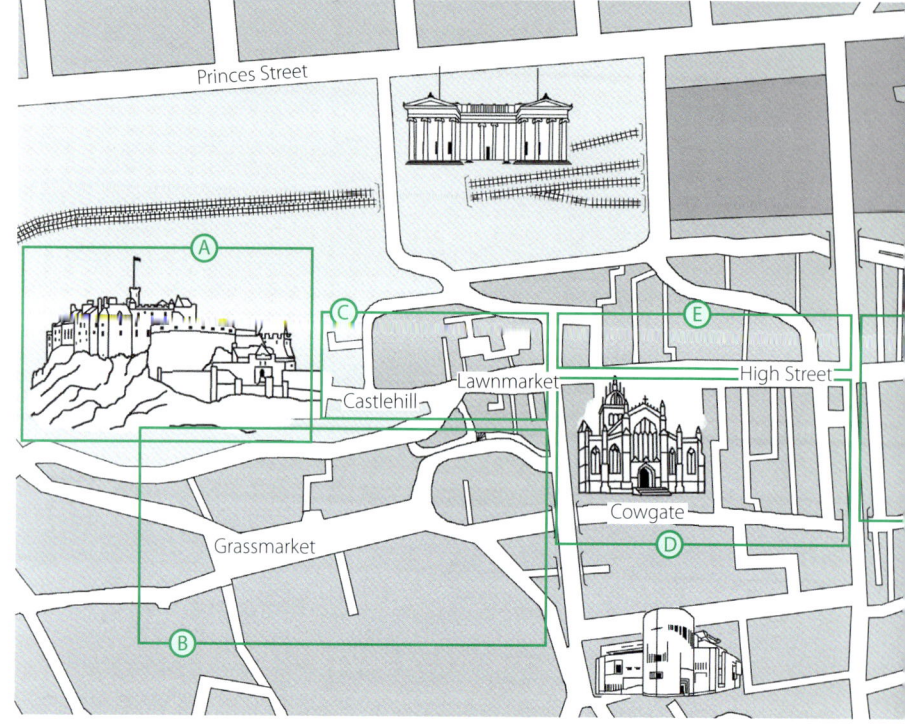

**THE OLD TOWN**

A   Edinburgh Castle
B   Below the Castle
C   Castlehill and Lawnmarket
D   Upper High Street (South Side)

E   Upper High Street (North Side)
F   Lower High Street
G   Canongate
H   Palace of Holyroodhouse and Abbey

those of highest status, for example the St Pol mansion:

> *It was a handsome, two-storeyed house with a thatched roof and a curved outside stair. It was built facing the causeway, on the slope of Castle Hill, with behind it a long, shelving garden.* (Gem, Pt 1, Ch 3)

Commonly, an outside stair led to living quarters above locked booths or luckenbooths at street level. These were shops where merchants and artisans could sell their wares.

In the 15th and 16th centuries there were around eighty closes in Edinburgh and this complex arrangement of passageways gave the advantage of home ground for Lymond when he is avoiding pursuit in the final chapter of *The Disorderly Knights*:

> *But Francis Crawford had the night on his side. He knew every wynd and vennel in Edinburgh, and provided in those first seconds he had obtained the lead he required,*

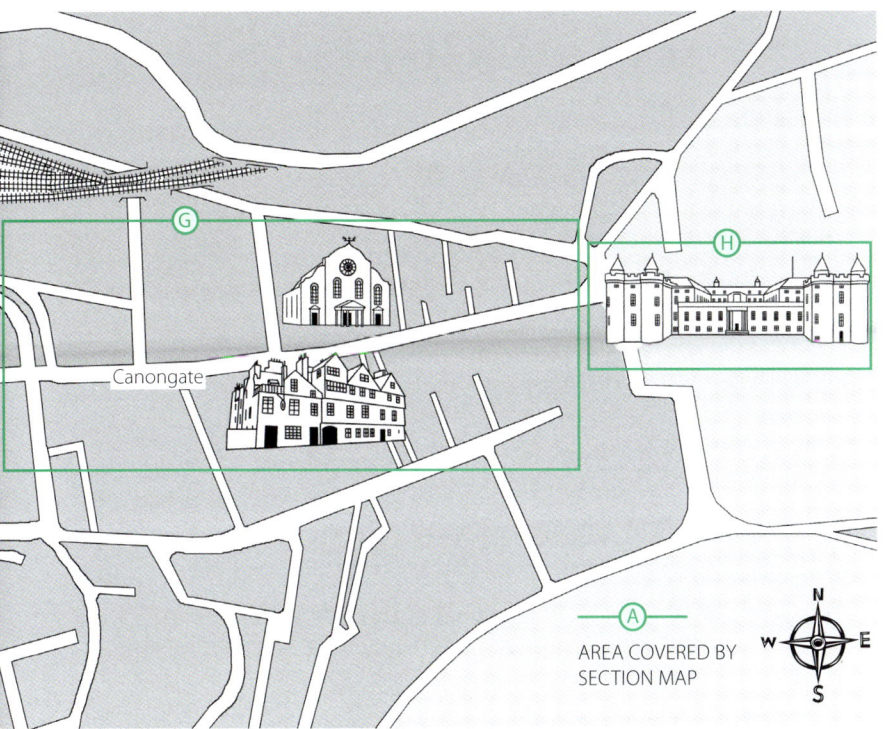

*he had at least a chance of escape. (DK, Pt 3, Ch 17)*

Edinburgh is not unique in having passageways dictated by geographical features. In *Checkmate*, the traboules of Lyons became the backdrop for pursuit. These convoluted pathways to the river crossed properties much like the closes of Edinburgh. Lymond says to Jerott:

*'Anyone who has visited Edinburgh knows about traboules.' (CM, Pt 1, Ch 6)*

Gelis recalls the effects of Edinburgh's geography whilst living in Antwerp:

*... the spiny ridges of Edinburgh, the funnelled views, the shrill winds. (TLWL, Pt 4, Ch 31)*

With pressure on space many closes have disappeared altogether. Others are now private but many remain to give today's visitors a taste of how the characters in the books experienced them.

# Locations

## A The Castle

> *Across four hundred feet of black lake, friezelike on their ridge, towered the houses of Edinburgh. Tonight the Castle on its pinnacle was fully lit, laying constellations on the water ...* (GoK, Opening Gambit)

Throughout the history of Edinburgh the Castle Rock has been a stronghold. Even in the modern city, the castle still dominates the skyline for miles. From its walls the view over all the surrounding land is spectacular, and lends even the visitor a sense of mastery over the landscape. Nothing conjures up an image of Edinburgh and perhaps of Scotland more than the Castle brooding on sheer rock.

In the 15th and 16th centuries the Castle's footprint was smaller and the entrance was higher up the rock, narrower and more defensible with a much steeper approach than today. It is within this smaller Castle that visitors can find the locations of both David's Tower and the round Constable's Tower. David's Tower features as a royal residence in The House of Niccolò, and as a prison in The Lymond Chronicles.

> *David's Tower ... was sixty feet high, rising above the wall and all other buildings, just as the Castle itself stood nearly three hundred feet above the deep valley around its three sides. The outer side of the curtain wall was quite sheer.* (TLWL, Pt 2, Ch 11)

The current Castle has three levels, called the Lower, Middle and Upper Wards. The medieval Castle occupied only the Upper Ward on the peak of the Castle Rock and at the time of the books the Middle Ward was outside the Castle wall. Today visitors enter the Lower Ward from the Castle Esplanade, which dates back in its current form to the 18th century. Excavations in 2010 revealed that beneath the Esplanade lie the remains of a 16th-century spur or defensive bastion, which added a further layer of protection to the Castle. The area was also used as a place of execution.

On entering the Castle look up and to your left as you walk along the path leading to Portcullis Gate at the great curving wall of the Half Moon Battery, which lies over the ruins of David's Tower. The curtain wall that runs between this and the site of the Constable's Tower is where the football match in *To Lie With Lions* was held, as detailed below.

### 1 Portcullis Gate (Constable's Tower)

This defensive gateway was built to replace the Constable's Tower which was the main gatehouse into the castle until it was badly damaged in 1573 in the Lang Siege. The upper storey was added later. Through this lies the Middle Ward, which was an industrial and service area in the 15th century.

### 2 Lang Stairs

Immediately to the left as you pass through the Portcullis Gate is the Lang Stairs. This is a steep set of 70 steps, which formed part of the original route to the peak of the Castle

#### A EDINBURGH CASTLE
1  Portcullis Gate (site of the Constable's Tower)
2  Lang Stairs
3  St Margaret's Chapel
4  Mons Meg
5  Forewall Battery (site of football pitch)
6  Half Moon Battery (site of David's Tower)
7  Crown Square (Palace Yard)
8  The Royal Palace
9  The Great Hall
10 Prisons of War

Rock. It would have led through the Constable's Tower into the Castle. Parts of the Tower have been found in the curving wall to the right of the stair and others excavated to the left of the Portcullis Gate. An alternative, less arduous route is via the roadway through the Middle Ward, built to accommodate the transport of large guns. It leads through the 17th-century Foogs Gate to Upper Ward.

### 3 St Margaret's Chapel
This is the oldest building in Edinburgh. It was built in 1130 by David I in honour of his

mother Queen Margaret, later St Margaret. Granddaughter to Edmund II of England, Margaret was the second wife of Malcolm III, known as Canmore, who emerged as king of Scotland by the end of *King Hereafter*. The chapel is tiny and was originally a private place of worship for the early medieval royal family. It is a beautiful space, enhanced by the original chevroned arch. By the 16th century, however, it was used as a store for gunpowder. It was eventually reclaimed and restored as a chapel, and the stained glass windows of St Andrew, St Ninian, St Columba, St Margaret and William Wallace are 20th century. It is still used for christenings and weddings.

### 4 Mons Meg

This six tonne siege gun was presented to James II of Scotland in 1457 by Duke Philip of Burgundy. James II had a keen interest in artillery, and during his reign these weapons were stored near the Palace Yard in the Castle when not in use. Mons Meg was used in the siege of Roxburgh Castle in 1460 where a similar gun exploded and cost James II his life. Readers will recognise this latter flawed gun as 'Mad Martha', which descended temporarily to the bottom of the canal at Damme after an unfortunate incident with the Duke of Burgundy's bath:

> ... *the Duke's cargo that sank was a gift – a gift from Duke Philip of Burgundy to his dear nephew James, King of Scotland. A fifteen-foot gift of some import. To be plain, a five-ton war cannon, grimly christened Mad Martha.* (NR, Ch 1)

Mons Meg continued in military service until 1550 when she was semi-retired into ceremonial use. The celebratory shot for the marriage of Mary, Queen of Scots to the French Dauphin from Edinburgh Castle reached Wardie Muir, the site of today's Botanic Gardens.

### 5 Forewall Battery (The 'football pitch')

You are now at the top of the wall you saw earlier from the Lower Ward. This is the line of the medieval exterior curtain wall, which ran between the two towers.

> *David's Tower at the south end was sixty feet high, rising above the wall and all other buildings, just as the Castle itself stood nearly three hundred feet above the deep valley around its three sides. The outer side of the curtain wall was quite sheer.* (TLWL, Pt 2, Ch 11)

Walking along past the 19th-century guns, you can pace the length of the 'football pitch' from the position of Constable's Tower at the top of the Lang Stairs to the position of David's Tower at the Half Moon Battery.

> *Black against the sky, the tall rectangle of the royal palace called David's Tower rose at one end, all its windows now lit, while far at the other end rose the round tower known as the Constable's, guarding the staircase to the inner citadel. But the top of the wall running between was quite dark, except where its crenellations blocked out the stars, and the forms of young men running along it.* (TLWL, Pt 2, Ch 11)

In Nicholas's time there was no wide platform for guns as now. This gun emplacement was originally built in the 1540s when the medieval wall was rebuilt a few years before Lymond's return to Edinburgh at the beginning of *The Game of Kings*. Although it was remodelled again after the Lang Siege with a higher interior ground level, it would have occupied a similar position in Lymond's day. In Nicholas's time, the ground level inside the Castle was lower and the curtain wall between the two towers appeared much taller than now so that an observer in the 15th century would have looked up at the match of Florentine football in *To Lie With Lions*. On the outside, the wall looked down on to bare rock:

> *[Kathi said] 'I gather we are having a game of Florentine football on the parapet, six a side instead of twenty-seven.' ... The curtain wall of Edinburgh Castle was four hundred feet long and twenty-four feet in height, with a sheer drop of another thirty-odd feet on the outside. The top was wide enough to take culverin, or three people running abreast, and the inner side was lined with interesting roof-tops. It made an irresistible playing field for two teams.* (TLWL, Pt 2, Ch 11)

### 6 Half Moon Battery (David's Tower)

Thirty metres tall, David's Tower was built for and named after David II. It was demolished during the Lang Siege and the Half Moon Battery, a semi circular wall with gun ports now lies in its place. It is possible to view all that remains of the ground floor of the Tower entombed within the Battery. These much altered vaulted chambers were converted into barracks in the late 16th century.

The football match ends in a draw so the winner has to be decided:

> *'... by trial of single combat. His grace the King and M. de Fleury are to race one another to the top of David's Tower'.* (TLWL, Pt 2, Ch 12)

The winner is to light the beacon fire on the roof of the tower. Robin climbs too, because he knows the footholds better and rescues both of them when they get into trouble on the climb. James claims victory and lights the fire.

For centuries David's Tower was the principal royal residence in the Castle. Nicholas is received there by the king after he returns from Iceland:

> *At the Castle, [Nicholas] was taken immediately to the monarch's private apartments in David's Tower. He was received in the room with the canopied chair and grandiose fireplace,*

Half Moon Battery

*generally used to impress personal heralds and foreign magnates of the medium rank.* (TLWL, Pt 4, Ch 30)

Towards the end of *Gemini*, the court is gathered in the Castle, probably in the Tower:

*From the windows of the audience chamber, looking down and abroad upon the silver links of the Forth, the flowery plain, the hills of the Highlands in the distance …* (Gem, Pt 5, Ch 45)

By Lymond's time, it had been superseded as a princely residence by the royal apartments in Crown Square (Palace Yard) but was still in use, on occasion, as accommodation for high-ranking prisoners. For instance, in *The Game of Kings*, Lymond starts his imprisonment here before being moved to the Tolbooth:

*… Lymond … being in ward in Her Majesty's Castle of Edinburgh, was summoned to … answer charges of treason …* (GoK, Pt 4, Ch 4)

Shortly afterwards it is the site of Will Scott's game of tarocco with Sir Thomas Palmer, who is held there after his capture by Buccleuch:

*The room in David's Tower was suffocatingly crowded … At [Sir Thomas Palmer's] request, he and a dozen of his own men had been put together in one medium sized room in the Castle […] a small-paned window looking sheer down the Castle rock into the loch, and a low, thick door with an adequate guard outside it.* (GoK, Pt 4, Ch 4)

## 7 Crown Square (Palace Yard)

In the 15th and 16th centuries this square at the peak of the Castle Rock was known as Palace Yard. It was extended during the reign of James III and building around it was begun then.

*The crown of the Castle rock, on which the royal lodgings were built, was not large, but many people lived in its towers, and crammed the lower offices that crowded round the hall, the chapel, the arsenal and the barracks, the archery ground and the stables. Ringed by its stout walls, the Castle of Edinburgh stood above the smoke and noise of the town, and its own smoke and noise affected only itself and the angels, which was fortunate.* (TLWL, Pt 2, Ch 11)

James III had vaults built into the rock (see 10, below) and created the platform on which Crown Square stands. Until that time the main buildings lay on the north-eastern part of the Castle Rock, with St Mary's, the Castle's main church, on the northern edge of the summit, whilst David's Tower and the Royal Palace stood on the eastern crags. The crag fell away steeply to the south-west down to the tilt yard (tournament ground) and James III's platform evened this ground. Buildings in the Square were situated along the four sides and gave some shelter from the winds that batter the Castle Rock: the Royal Palace, the Great Hall, St Mary's Church and the Royal Gunhouse.

The Royal Palace

By the time of The Lymond Chronicles, the Royal Palace, on the east side, was the principal royal residence, although Holyrood Palace was also favoured by the royal family. The Great Hall on the south was complete and St Mary's Church on the north was being used as an armoury. The Royal Palace and the Great Hall remain but St Mary's Church has been replaced by the National War Memorial, and the Royal Gunhouse by the 18th-century Queen Anne Building.

**8 The Royal Palace**

The Royal Palace began life as an extension to David's Tower during the reign of James I, and was enlarged by subsequent monarchs, with significant work starting in the reign of James III. His palace still remains, although was substantially renovated during the reign of James VI and new rooms created. The current restoration reflects this later remodelling. One tiny room is identified as James VI's birthplace, and the rooms are richly decorated with royal portraits.

Sandy Albany escapes from here in 1479, after returning from making trouble in the Borders. In *Gemini* Nicholas is involved in his return to Edinburgh.

> *Sandy was locked into his own rooms, tired but happy; Liddell and Nicholas were put in the spare chart-room, which was at the top of David's Tower. [...]*
>
> *Alexander, Duke of Albany, escaped, with the help of his excitable brother, just as soon as it dawned on him that he was not in course of receiving a rap on the knuckles, but was about to be incarcerated for some considerable time. In the guise of a grim, long-nosed woman, he rode out of the Castle with Johndie Mar and down to Leith, where a small boat waited to take him out to a larger.* (Gem, Pt 2, Ch 22)

Above the ground-floor window at the corner of the Royal Palace and the Great Hall is set a plaque commemorating the death of Mary de Guise in the castle in 1560, before her body was transported to Rheims.

The Honours of Scotland comprise the Crown, Sceptre and Sword of State, which were formerly held in David's Tower and are now all on display in the Royal Palace. They and the Stone of Destiny are displayed with a description of their eventful history.

Of particular interest to Dorothy Dunnett readers is the crown that was made for James V in 1540 by John Mossman, an Edinburgh Goldsmith. It was first worn by James V at the coronation of Mary de Guise at Holyrood Abbey. Mary, Queen of Scots was crowned with this crown as an infant, and it can be seen as symbolic of her rule, but it was left at home by the Commissioners when they attended her wedding to the Dauphin:

> *A crown was having to be made [for the wedding] because the Scottish Commissioners, to everyone's surprise and annoyance, had failed to bring with them the Scottish Crown Matrimonial for use at the ceremony, and refused to send for it. (CM, Pt 3, Ch 5)*

The Crown of Scotland, in this context, was symbolic of the Crown Matrimonial, the legal device that would have given Mary's husband the right to rule jointly with her, and as king if he outlived her.

### 9 The Great Hall

The Great Hall was built during the reign of James IV in 1511, and remains an imposing space taking up one side of Crown Square. It was used as a barracks by Oliver Cromwell's troops, and remained so until the 19th century, when it was restored. The walls bristle with a collection of weaponry and armour, and the Hall owes its stained glass to the 19th-century restoration. It is, however, topped by an exquisite hammer beam roof, whose stone corbels are carved with the arms of James IV, and are the earliest such examples in Britain.

### 10 Prisons of War (Vaults)

This series of chambers runs underneath the buildings in Crown Square and essentially form their foundations. Built during the reign of James III, these chambers were used as prisons over many centuries and nowadays provide an atmospheric exhibition space.

## B Below the Castle

### 11 The Grassmarket

The Grassmarket lies in a hollow below the Castle Rock and the ridge of the Royal Mile.

When Nicholas walks through the Grassmarket, or Horse Market, it was the principal market for livestock in Edinburgh and since James II's reign the only place in Edinburgh where live animals could be sold. He makes his way into the city via the Cowgate:

> *The Horse Market was, of course, always thronged. A wide, muddy space lined with houses, today it was full of heralds, competitors, workmen, horse-copers, drinkers and merchant friends and merchant competitors. To the left rose the black basalt rock of the Castle. On the right, among the private houses, the taverns, and the chapels was the house of St John and the opulent monastery of the Franciscans, whose buildings covered the rise which led towards the Port to the common. Tomorrow, after the joust, the Eve of St Nicholas Feast would be held in the monastery and he, Nicholas de Fleury, would be there. But there was a great deal to do before that. (UH, Pt 1, Ch 5)*

Today, the area is no longer muddy, but still retains the air of a wide market place, which occasionally accommodates markets or entertainment. The house of St John lay on the south side of the street, just west of Hunter's Close, but the buildings were demolished in the 19th century.

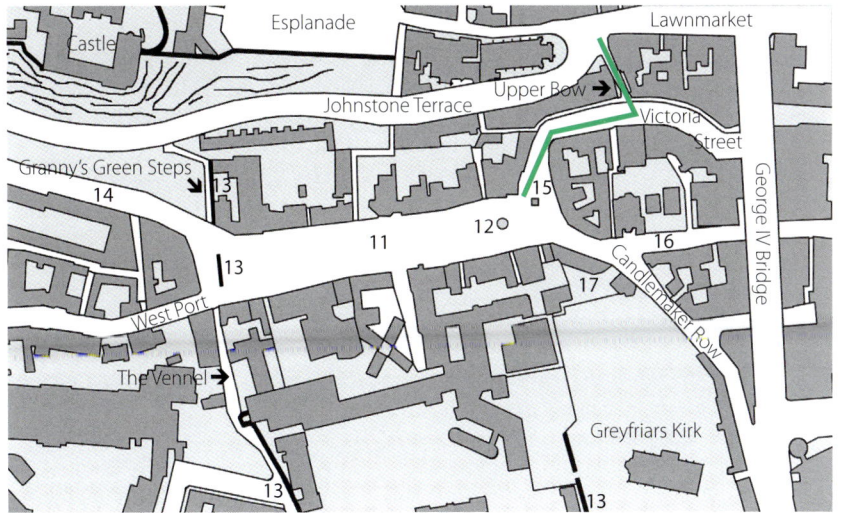

## B BELOW THE CASTLE

11  The Grassmarket
12  Covenanter's Memorial (Newbygging)
13  The Flodden Wall
14  Site of Tournament Grounds
15  West Bow
16  The Cowgate
17  Site of Greyfriars Monastery
━  Original route of West Bow

### 12 Covenanters' Memorial (Newbygging)

The Grassmarket was also called Newbygging and was a place of execution. After Hexham, Buccleuch gives his opinion on Lymond's probable fate on his return to Edinburgh:

> 'Oh. Well, he's at the horn, isn't he? It'll be the Castle then, I dare say, for a week or two; and then a sweet short trial and a swing in New Bigging Street. Nothing surer than that.' (GoK, Pt 4, Ch 3)

The site of the public gallows is marked by a circular grey granite memorial, the Covenanters' Memorial.

### 13 The Flodden Wall (Granny's Green Steps, the Vennel and West Port)

The Flodden Wall is commemorated in the paving stones that run through the pedestrian area at the western end between two closes that climb up the steep sides of the deep valley: the Vennel (to the south) and Granny's Green Steps (to the north). Both are bounded on their eastern side by sections of the wall and the only surviving guard tower can be seen in the upper portion of the Vennel. Just beyond it, the Flodden Wall merges with the 17th-century Telfer Wall extension.

The West Port, a gate that existed at least by 1437, was incorporated into the Flodden Wall and became the main south-western gate. It is commemorated in the street so-named at the south-western corner of the Grassmarket.

## 14 Tournament Grounds

King's Stables Road is in the north-west corner of the Grassmarket. Near here were the lists or tournament grounds somewhere between West Port and Castle Rock. The area has been extensively remodelled and, whilst it is still dominated by the crag, the modern buildings make it hard to see where the ground would have been flat enough for a set of lists.

It is here, outside the wall, that the two tournaments that feature in *The Unicorn Hunt* take place: the Tournament of the Unicorn, where Nicholas is stabbed, and the *joust à plaisance* for Margaret of Denmark's arrival. The stands are set up differently for each. At the Tournament of the Unicorn:

> *[Kathi was] wrapped in her thickest cloak against the wind that scoured down upon her from the face of the Castle, and the smoke that swirled ... round her from the braziers and bonfires round the tiltground.*
>
> *To one side, grafted on to the lower ledges of rock was the long pavilion, its canvas snapping and belching ...*
>
> *Behind [Nicholas] stretched the green grass of the lists, all one hundred and fifty yards of it, and a third as wide. On one long side facing the Rock stood the mass of the common spectators ...* (UH, Pt 1, Ch 6)

For Margaret of Denmark:

> *The stands ... were two-tiered, built to face one another across the width of the lists, so that the royal party gazed at the Rock and its lesser guests sat with their backs to it. The royal pavilion was hung with cloth of gold and lined with velvet and tassels: and the knights' tents at one end were all stitched in silk with the banners crowded around them, catching the afterglow from the west.* (UH, Pt 1, Ch 21)

## 15 West Bow

This Z-shaped street climbed from the Grassmarket to the Lawnmarket, up a steep incline that led from the Bow Foot to the Bow Head, through the West or Upper Bow port in the King's Wall. It was originally so steep that traders attempting to push handcarts or other goods often had to zigzag along the street. Houses were so tightly packed together that it was later said that people could drink tea with their neighbours on the opposite side of the street without having to leave their homes.

Today, West Bow leads into Victoria Street and thence to George IV Bridge (both constructed in the 19th century), which has a gentler, but by no means easy, curved incline.

Victoria Terrace runs above the level of Victoria Street, forming a picturesque second tier of shops. To follow the original route of the West Bow into Edinburgh more closely, turn left into a narrow set of stairs just before the point where the terrace develops round arches. At their head you will arrive at the Upper Bow, which is where the West Bow used to decant into the Lawnmarket. An information board gives the story of the street at this point. If you want to avoid the stairs you can follow Victoria Street to its end, and approach from the Lawnmarket.

Nicholas walks from the preparation for the Tournament of the Unicorn through Grassmarket up the steep street to Kilmirren House:

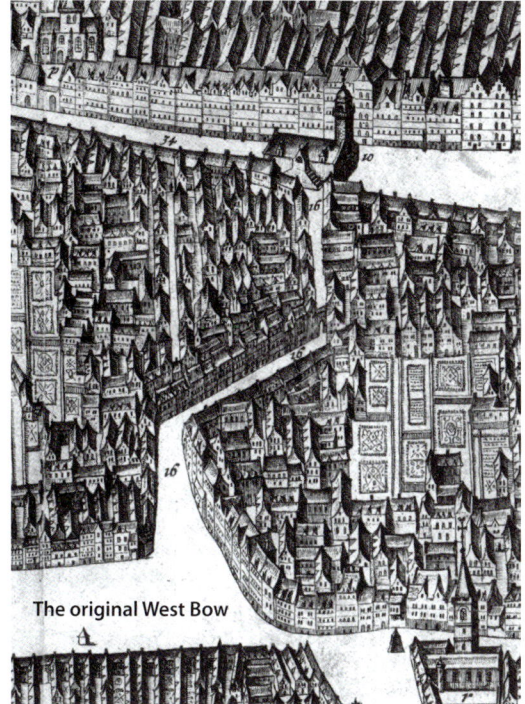

The original West Bow

*The quickest way there from the tilting-ground was through the broad space of the Horse Market and up the steep dog-leg path to the High Street. And on the other side of that street was ... [t]he Edinburgh house of the St Pol of Kilmirren ... He stopped and talked to perhaps twenty people on his way to the Bow ... He was at the top of the Bow.* (UH, Pt 1, Ch 5)

The West or Upper Bow gate was situated near the upper bend of the Z, where the modern West Bow becomes Victoria Street, and led to landward routes within Scotland. It remained as a second level of defence when the Flodden Wall was built.

The Kerrs, and then Lymond, come this way on the night of Buccleuch's death:

*[Lymond, Jerott and Sir James Sandilands], the Grand Prior's train of twelve men-at-arms riding behind them, swept up to and through the Bow gates, and cantering up the steep slopes to Castle Hill, deployed down the street.* (DK, Pt 3, Ch 17)

### 16 The Cowgate

The Cowgate runs below and parallel to the whole length of the High Street, the two connected by a number of closes. Jordan de Ribérac owns a house on the Cowgate as does Martin of the Vatachino and James Liddell. During the Renaissance it was a very desirable address. In 1550 Alexander Alesse wrote of it: 'where the nobility and chief men of the city reside and in which are the palaces of the officers of state and where nothing is mean and tasteless, but all is magnificent.' Kathi certainly recognises it as an up-and-coming area when she walks up towards the High Street:

*[Kathi] liked the Cowgate. It used to be full of rubbish and dung, but as the city spilled outside its walls, tumbling down from the ridge to the long ravine on this, its south side, the richer families and wealthier churchmen began to build [there] ... The Clerk Register's house was on the rising ground at that end of the Cowgate, close to that of James Liddell, where Julius obediently spent so much of his time.* (Gem, Pt 4, Ch 37)

Today it is a deep canyon of tall buildings.

### 17 Greyfriars Monastery

Candlemaker Row leads steeply uphill from the corner of Cowgate and the Grassmarket towards Greyfriars Kirk. The Franciscan church and friary buildings occupied the sloping ground there from 1458 until they were destroyed by Protestant reformers in 1559.

In *The Unicorn Hunt* the banquets that followed the two tournaments are both held there.

> *As ever, the Greyfriars' hospitality was excellent, and the food and entertainment first class. The choir performed twice, and there were jesters and jugglers and mountebanks, followed by a short play.* (UH, Pt 1, Ch 7)

> *The royal procession had gone to the Greyfriars whose establishment, as memory served, was the only one qualified to contain so large and prestigious a company.* (UH, Pt 1, Ch 22)

The position of the original church at the corner has long been built over. However, access to Greyfriars Kirk lies further up Candlemaker Row on the right. The kirk was built in 1620, the first in Edinburgh after the Reformation. The kirkyard was granted to the citizens of Edinburgh by Mary, Queen of Scots in 1562 as a burial ground, when the one at St Giles' became too crowded, and it became desirable to bury the dead further from the centre of the city. A section of the Flodden Wall can be seen in the kirkyard.

Many famous and noteworthy Edinburgh individuals are buried here, and there is a monument to the 17th-century Covenanters, Protestant reformers and successors to the Lords of the Congregation who were imprisoned in a field that is now part of the kirkyard. Perhaps the smallest grave belongs to Greyfriars Bobby, a devoted dog who guarded his master's grave and has a statue in his honour at the top of Candlemaker Row. Just across the main road from the statue is the National Museum of Scotland and to the right, at the back of the museum, is the cul-de-sac bearing the name of the Bristo Port. This gate was used by Lymond when he rode with Adam Acheson to Berwick:

> *Next morning Lymond, swordless, left Edinburgh's Bristo Port with a courier carrying Sir George's letters and Sir George's safe-conduct.* (GoK, Pt 4, Ch 2)

## C Castlehill (Castle Hill) and Lawnmarket

Castlehill is the modern name for Castle Hill, the steep part of the Royal Mile leading downhill from the Esplanade. At one point it was an expensive and desirable place to live, with royalty the nearest neighbours. The road widens and changes its name to the Lawnmarket as it meets Johnston Terrace and the Upper Bow at a mini-roundabout.

The Lawnmarket is named for the 'inland market' or 'land market' that took place there, with stalls and traders selling wares made in Scotland. It gradually became associated with trade in cloth, and gained a charter from James III in 1477. The Lawnmarket ends at the crossroads with Bank Street and George IV Bridge. The locations described

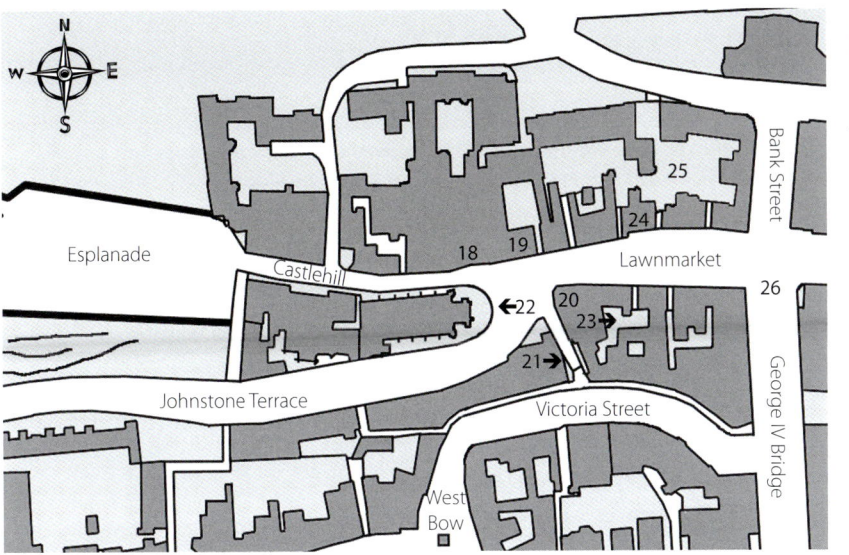

### C CASTLEHILL (CASTLE HILL) AND LAWNMARKET
18  Site of Mary de Guise's Palace
19  Site of Kilmirren House
20  Site of Nicholas's House
21  Upper Bow
22  Site of Butter Tron
23  Riddles Court
24  Gladstone's Land
25  Makars' Court and the Writers' Museum
26  Site of Mungo Tennant's House

below lay within the boundaries of the King's Wall.

### 18 Mary de Guise's Palace
The final scenes of *The Game of Kings* take place here.

> *In Mary de Guise's palace the tapers took fire from room to room, as the Queen Dowager moved with her maids to the audience chamber, turning her head as she walked to speak to Richard, on her right, and Henry Lauder, behind her.* (GoK, Pt 4, Ch 4)

The palace was on the north side of the road at the point where Castlehill becomes the Lawnmarket, and Mary de Guise lived here during her regency for her daughter. Her residence spread out over three closes, and included reception rooms, living quarters and a private oratory. A garden stretched down to the Nor' Loch and there was a hidden route into and out of the palace within one of the closes for those requiring subterfuge.

In succeeding centuries, the house was broken up into smaller dwellings and, like much of the Old Town, fell into disrepair. When it was demolished in 1845 some of the Renaissance decoration remained. Original ornately carved stone and wooden panels are displayed in the National Museum of Scotland. The General Assembly Hall of the

Church of Scotland now stands on the site.

Mary de Guise arranges the longed-for reunion between Lymond and his mother in her palace.

> *In a lifetime of empty rooms, this was another. Then there was a whisper of silk, a perfume half remembered, a humane, quizzical, intuitive presence; and a wild relief that deluged the tired and passionate mind. Sybilla was there. She saw her son's eyes, and flung open her arms.* (GoK, Pt 4, Ch 4)

### 19 Kilmirren House

The St Pol Edinburgh home and Nicholas's leased house in *Gemini* are described as diagonally opposite one another. The former was on the north side of Castlehill and the latter on the south side of the Lawnmarket, both very close to the place where the road changes its name. This would place Kilmirren House near or perhaps even on one of the three closes that subsequently formed Mary de Guise's palace and were later subsumed into the Church of Scotland General Assembly Hall. The position of the St Pol house is pinpointed when Nicholas goes there during the preparation for the Tournament of the Unicorn. As he climbs the Bow, Dorothy Dunnett notes that:

> *Kilmirren House was on Castle Hill, at the place where the upper end of the High Street began to climb the increasing slope to the Castle itself.* (UH, Pt 1, Ch 5)

When he gets there he meets Bel:

> *... [it] was in the best site in town but not extravagant in its fittings. The parlour she sat in was decent, with a good timber ceiling, a few kists, a few stools, some canvas hangings and a board with some silver and pewter laid out on it. The house itself was of two storeys only, of white-plastered timber, and thatched.* (UH, Pt 1, Ch 5)

Slightly further up Castlehill is the intriguingly named Semple Close, but this owes its name to the 17th-century Lady Semple, who had a mansion at its foot, rather than any of Dorothy Dunnett's protagonists.

### 20 Nicholas's House

The house Nicholas leases in *Gemini* is near the head of today's Upper Bow. That street now opens into the beginning of Johnston Terrace. In Nicholas's time the West Bow decanted directly into the junction of Castle Hill and Lawnmarket and the house would have been at or near that corner. The Kilmirren House would have been across the road and slightly uphill.

> *... the spacious, timber house near the head of the Bow, with its service buildings and stable behind, in the terraced ground that plunged down to the Cowgate. It was on the opposite side of the road from Kilmirren House, Henry's home, and a shade further away from the Castle.* (Gem, Pt 1, Ch 7)

> *[Nicholas] had described the house ... It was timber and tall, and stood near the*

*The West Bow from the Lawnmarket, 1829*

Bow, past where the High Street merged into the Lawnmarket. Because of its site, it had been expensive, and he had taken care to explain why it was necessary. *(Gem, Pt 1, Ch 11)*

Other characters also have homes in the Lawnmarket though their exact locations are not given.

Sir George Douglas's lodging is in the Lawnmarket and when Lymond leaves there with Douglas's letters and safe conduct to redeem Christian Stewart by surrendering to Lord Grey:

*The day was breathless with promise; the cobbles shining like milk glass in the quiet; the gables asleep in blanket rolls of mist. (GoK, Pt 4, Ch 2)*

George Paris, the double agent in *The Disorderly Knights* has lodgings there, and the Kerrs search his rooms for incriminating papers before murdering Wat Scott.

## 21 Upper Bow

Upper Bow is the top part of West Bow, the steep street connecting the Royal Mile with the Grassmarket. It is one of the roads that converge on the mini-roundabout where Castlehill becomes the Lawnmarket. Lymond uses this route into the city when attempting to intercept Buccleuch and the Kerrs:

*Lymond ... took the direct route to the West Bow, to bring him quickly into the Lawnmarket where George Paris was lodged. (DK, Pt 3, Ch 17)*

Johnston Terrace was built in the 19th century and skims the south side of Castle Rock from the same roundabout. From further down the street there are attractive views of the city and the Castle.

Somewhere below here at the base of the Castle Rock were the lists or tournament grounds.

## 22 The Hub (Site of the Butter Tron)

*Rumour of the hurried Assize had reached the streets by midday, and by two o'clock the Lawnmarket from the Butter Tron to St Giles was thick with people. (GoK, Pt 4, Ch 4, 2)*

A tron was a public weighing scale used to check the weights of goods entering the city so that they could be taxed appropriately. Surviving machines worked using a beam mounted on a pillar, and the name comes from the French *tronel* or *troneau* meaning balance. Each area would have its own because, until the 17th century, Scotland did not have a single standard set of weights and measures. The Butter Tron was housed in a building that stood near the site now occupied by the 19th-century Highland Tolbooth Church of St John. This church has been deconsecrated and is now used during the Edinburgh Festival as a venue and box office named the Hub.

### 23 RIDDLES COURT
On the south side of the road lies Riddles Court. It does not appear in the books but it is a splendid (and photogenic) example of a 16th-century fortified house. Now restored as the Patrick Geddes Centre, it has limited opening hours to the public. A 16th-century decorative plastered ceiling hints at the grandeur that once hosted a royal banquet for James VI.

### 24 GLADSTONE'S LAND
This distinctive house has a model pig in a trough by the door and an external stair. The pig, which illustrates how closely citizens lived to their livestock, will remind readers of Mungo Tennant.

*He led the way to the apartment beneath the stairs where lived Mungo's great sow, the badge of his house, the pet and idiotic pig's apple of his eye, and waited while Hob Hewat filled its water trough. (GoK, Opening Gambit)*

Owned by the National Trust for Scotland, this tenement in the Lawnmarket has been restored, mostly as a 17th-century dwelling. The early part of the building, however, dates to 1550 and is built in the traditional style so offers insight into the layout and the feel of the lands. On the ground floor a cloth merchant's booth is constructed as a luckenbooth. There is also a display of shades and colours achieved by dyes of the period and their origins. Upstairs the rooms are mostly furnished in early 17th-century style not that far removed from Lymond's period. In the Painted Chamber there is a beautifully decorated original painted ceiling. The Green Room, although 18th century, has a fascinating model of the land as it developed over the centuries and a spinet (curiously restrained compared to the one in *Pawn in Frankincense*).

### 25 MAKARS' COURT AND THE WRITERS' MUSEUM
Lady Stair's Close and Wardrop's Court both lead to Makars' Court, where there is a memorial stone to Dorothy Dunnett, and the Writers' Museum. The museum is devoted to Scottish writers, with permanent displays about Sir Walter Scott, Robert Burns and Robert Louis Stevenson, and exhibitions about Scottish writing.

Just outside is Makars' Court in which the lives and works of Scottish writers are celebrated in flagstones, each inscribed with a quotation. The Scots word *makar* means a maker or creator, and has been used since the 15th century to describe writers or poets of particular skill. The first stone was unveiled in 1997, and the Dorothy Dunnett Society

Memorial Stone at Makars' Court

sponsored a stone in her memory in 2006. It is the focus of the Society's annual International Dorothy Dunnett Day gathering in Edinburgh. The stone lies just south of the doorway of the Writers' Museum, and bears a quotation from *Checkmate* that has particular resonance for her writing.

*Where are the links of the chain ... joining us to the past? (CM, Pt 4, Ch 9)*

## 26 Mungo Tennant's House

*In his tall house in Gosford Close with the boar's head in chief over the lintel.* (GoK, Opening Gambit)

Gosford Close lay, counter-intuitively, on the south side of the road very near to today's George IV Bridge. Previously known as Dickson's Close and earlier still as Aikman's Close, it demonstrates the Edinburgh habit of constantly renaming closes after notable residents. Mungo Tennant was a historical figure, a real and successful burgess of Edinburgh. His house was demolished along with Gosford Close in 1830 to make way for George IV Bridge.

During this work a cellar was discovered. It had a concealed trap door leading to another hidden cellar hewn out of the rock. Dorothy Dunnett described a long rock tunnel, which stretched all the way beneath the High Street and the houses opposite to the Nor' Loch. As a royal burgh, Edinburgh owned a monopoly on international trade of important goods, and the tunnel would have been a convenient way of avoiding the taxes charged at more conventional entrances to the city. Lymond used it for a different purpose:

*For where a smuggler's load could pierce a city's defences, so could an outlawed rebel, whose life would be forfeit if caught.* (GoK, Opening Gambit)

The house also appears in *Gemini*. In the 15th century Gosford Close was named Aikman's Close, and the house was in the possession of the Augustinian Priory of Cambuskenneth. Nicholas visits Abbot Henry there where the same double cellar with its nefarious purpose is described:

*'And since you are going,' said Abbot Henry, 'you might place us all in your debt by*

*taking a few crates to a warehouse? The goods may be removed from here by night. It is an old smugglers' route. The cellar tunnel leads to the Nor' Loch. We discovered it when we acquired the house for the monastery.' (Gem, Pt 4, Ch 35)*

## The High Street

The High Street was the main hub of commerce in Edinburgh in the 15th and 16th centuries and parliament, the courts and prisons were also here. St Giles', then a Collegiate Church, stood at the heart of this community and features particularly in *The Disorderly Knights*. Although the street is now relatively clear for our modern traffic, prior to the 19th century the road was much narrower, buildings jutted out into the thoroughfare and it would have bustled with activity:

*Nicholas and Anselm Adorne walked ... [along] the High Street; impeded as ever by the onslaught of eager bodies who wished to sell something, or extract news or impart it, or establish a personal forum on a question of public importance. Fresh from the sea, it was a change to be among pigs, and horseflies, and children; and banging from the hammermen's shops, and disputatious clamour from packed, busy markets. Every brosy face on the causeway had a name, or a nickname. (Gem, Pt 3, Ch 33)*

### Characters at Home in the High Street

Characters from both series have homes in the High Street, and in the upper part there are also several steeply descending closes on either side that are of interest to the Dorothy Dunnett reader. Nicholas and Gelis live in the High Street in *To Lie With Lions*.

*Gelis said. 'Where shall we stay? You have a pretty cassino, you once told me, in Edinburgh.' He had bought it for her, long ago. Long ago, before the day of their wedding. [Nicholas] said, 'I still have it. It is yours as soon as my tenants have moved.' (TLWL, Pt 1, Ch 8)*

The tenants are the Prioress of Haddington and her entourage, who move next door.

*[Kathi said to Gelis] We are only next door ... The Edinburgh house of the Priory ... When the Prioress couldn't find satisfactory premises, M. de Fleury bought the house next to this, and presented it to them. (TLWL, Pt 2, Ch 13)*

Clues to the location are given when Nicholas walks from his house to the Kilmirren house, passing St Giles', and help us place it somewhere downhill of the church. There is a possible implication that it lies on the south side of the street.

*The house of Jordan de Ribérac was quite close: between the top of the High Street and the Castle itself. To reach it, Nicholas had to traverse the busiest width of the road, including the graveyard and King's park of the church of St Giles, and the houses of well-doing burgesses. (TLWL, Pt 2, Ch 19)*

Anselm Adorne lives almost opposite Nicholas:

*In the High Street of Edinburgh, one of the few mansions unaffected by theatrical madness was that of Anselm Adorne ... The house of Nicholas, across the street, was – by his own decree – the centre of the whole enterprise of the Nativity. (TLWL, Pt 2, Ch 13)*

Houses for which Dorothy Dunnett has given us more clues are discussed in the locations below.

## D Upper High Street – South Side

### 27 The High Kirk of St Giles

St Giles' with its high stone crown spire dominates the upper section of the High Street. It sits today in Parliament Square and can be viewed from all sides, but this was not the case until the late 18th century. At the times the books are set, the Tolbooth and the Luckenbooths were buildings that clung closely to the church on its west and north sides so that the church was hardly visible from there. To its south the kirkyard extended down

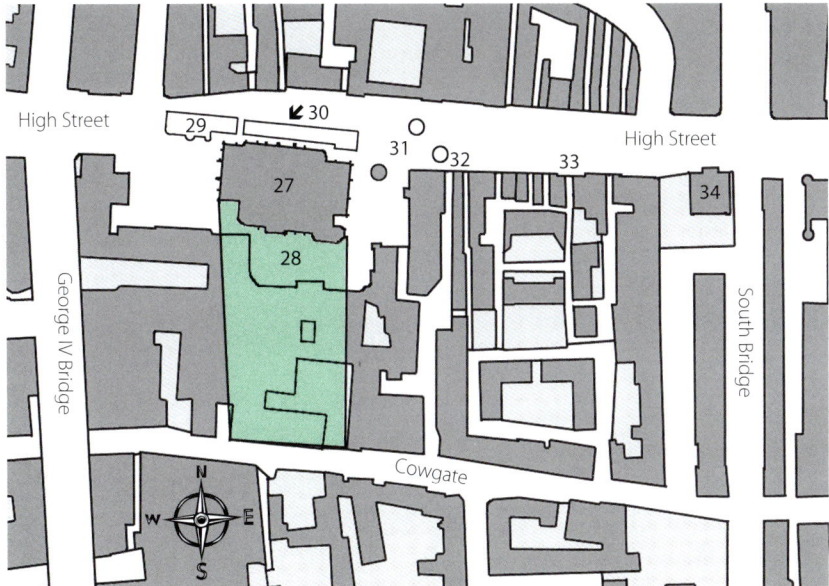

### D UPPER HIGH STREET – SOUTH SIDE

27   The High Kirk of St Giles
28   Parliament Square
29   Site of Tolbooth
30   Site of Luckenbooths
31   Mercat Cross, current and previous positions

32   Site of Conn's Close
33   Bell's Wynd
34   Tron Kirk (site of Buccleuch's House)
■   Area covered by St Giles' Kirkyard

The High Kirk of St Giles

a long slope to the Cowgate. The north porch gave on to the Stinkand Style, the narrow dark passageway between the Luckenbooths and the church. From the 15th century until the Reformation the church held a relic of St Giles, the history and provenance of which is referred to by Dorothy Dunnett in *Gemini*. It is brought to Tobie's mind during a visit to Roslin, as he ruminates about the families Sinclair and Preston.

> *A generation ago, a Sir William Preston of Craigmillar had brought back the armbone of St Giles for St Giles'. Bruges already had an armbone of St Giles in its St Giles'. Edinburgh was almost upsides with Bruges. One of these days, Edinburgh would be the equal of Bruges. Only Gibbie Fish, who fashioned the reliquary case, could have told them that both were left arms.* (Gem, Pt 2, Ch 17)

Preston, an antecedent of the Prestons of Craigmillar in *Gemini*, was buried in the Lady Aisle to the right of the high altar. To the right (south) of that aisle is the Preston Aisle, or chapel, named in honour of his donation, which has a particularly fine groined roof. The 19th-century neo-Gothic Thistle Chapel, the centre of the chivalric Order of the Thistle, leads off the Preston Aisle, which is hung with the banners of its members.

The new marble altar at the crossing in the middle of the church was dedicated in 2011, although repositioning of the sanctuary to the crossing first occurred in the 1980s. For most of the church's history, services were conducted from the east end of the church and the high altar lay between the last two easternmost pillars.

The 15th and 16th centuries saw a proliferation of side altars, funded by families or guilds, until by 1560 there were around fifty. There were rules around dedicating altars,

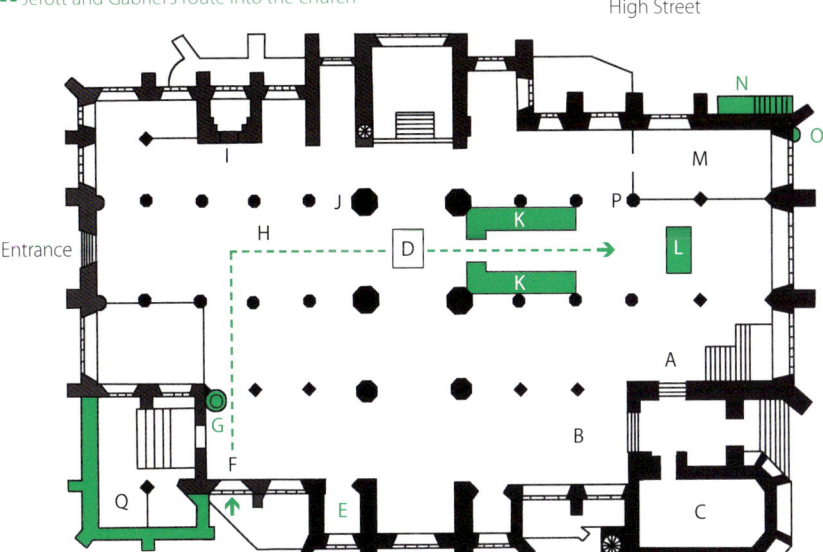

- Current features
- 16th-century features (sites of)
- Jerott and Gabriel's route into the church

High Street

Entrance

Parliament Square

**THE HIGH KIRK OF ST GILES**

- A Lady Aisle
- B Preston Aisle
- C Thistle Chapel
- D Holy Table (modern altar)
- E Holy Blood Chapel
- F Site of the South Door
- G Site of Font
- H Nave
- I Site of Norman porch (North Door)
- J Site of St Eloi's Chapel
- K Site of choir stalls
- L Site of High Altar
- M Holy Cross Aisle (Chapel of the Holy Cross)
- N Site of Lady Steps
- O Site of Virgin's Niche
- P Randy Bell's octagonal pillar
- Q Lauder's Chapel

which required permission from burgh authorities and bishop, and proof of a year's worth of funding. Banners decorated the church from these sponsors, often from guilds (individual trade incorporations).

> *The great choral responsory devised by Will Roger alone was performed before hundreds in the burgh's own High Kirk of St Giles, with the guilds and their flags standing each before its own altar. Dr Andreas arrayed himself with his flock before the glittering shrine of St Crispin ... (Gem, Pt 4, Ch 37)*

*From more than forty altars the long, white tapers pricked to life with their small flame the dim treasures of jewels and paintings, of silver-gilt and delicate, handsewn fabric and queer, painted faces that graced the aisles and chapels of the long two hundred foot nave, and lent their bouquet of light and incense to the rows of thick stone pillars that upheld the groined stone arches, far above.* (DK, Pt 3, Ch 17)

The Confraternity of the Holy Blood, founded in Bruges, dedicated one such altar in St Giles', which remains to this day on the south side of the church.

St Giles' Cathedral is the High Kirk of Edinburgh and the principal place of worship of the Church of Scotland in the city. Despite its importance in the history of Edinburgh, St Giles' was a Collegiate Church in the diocese of St Andrews and never a Catholic cathedral.

St Giles' became a Protestant (Presbyterian) church in 1560 during the Reformation. It was then that some of the icons, such as the statue and relic of St Giles, were lost or destroyed. Charles I made St Giles' a cathedral in the 17th century and provoked resentment and rioting when he attempted to change the liturgy to be more in line with that used in the Church of England.

Over the following centuries St Giles' was put to many uses, and at one point was subdivided into four separate churches. Restoration work took place in 1829, encasing the exterior of the church in smooth ashlar and demolishing several chapels. Further renovation took place in 1872–3.

St Giles' is the setting for the climactic scene of *The Disorderly Knights*, and the highlighted text traces the confrontation between Lymond and Gabriel.

### The Fight at the Altar – *The Disorderly Knights* (Pt 3, Ch 17)

*... side by side, their robes airy behind them, the two Knights of St John of Jerusalem climbed the wide steps, between the clustering lamps, and entered the great church of St Giles.*

Here is a guide for those wanting to retrace the final scene in *The Disorderly Knights*. Much of it is described in the novel from the point of view of Jerott Blyth.

He enters with Gabriel from the south door, through the porch, which was the traditional scene of weddings. Although this entrance is no longer there, its location can be found under a window depicting Moses and other Old Testament figures.

Jerott also notes the font where he was christened. Its position was close to the 20th-century memorial to Robert Louis Stevenson. He then turns right up the central nave towards the east end of the church and the high altar:

*He paced with Gabriel up the stone floor of the nave, past the Norman door, past the chapel where hung the Blue Blanket.*

The North Door in the 18th century

The Norman door would have been the north door leading to the Booth Raw. Its position was beneath the window showing Scottish saints. The Blue Blanket was the guilds' flag or standard, which was sponsored by the craft guilds of Edinburgh and is said to have been made by Queen Margaret, wife of James III. This was given by the king in 1482 in recognition of the role of the craftsmen in helping to free him from his incarceration in the Castle after the events at Lauder Bridge (see *Gem*, Pt 5, Ch 46). It was subsequently used to call the citizens of Edinburgh to arms and was brought back from the battlefield of Flodden in 1513 with the news of the Scots' defeat. It was housed in the Chapel of St Eloi, which at that time was situated at the north-west pillar of the crossing.

In passing, Jerott notes six more aisles and altars dedicated to saints, the organ and the finely carved choir stalls. Mary de Guise was a frequent visitor to St Giles' and brought in her own craftsman, Andrew Mansion, who created ornate carvings for the choir stalls and screens:

*Then [Jerott] could see the steps to the high altar, its chandeliers blazing with light; its vestments of black and red velvet and of cloth of gold; its pall of red satin hangings blatant in heraldic pattern behind ... For a moment [he] ... looked up at the painted face of the tall statue [of St Giles], vested in cloth of gold and red velvet pendicle, placed above the jewelled casket bearing his relic: a hand and armbone, drily anonymous, with a diamond ring rattling loose on its finger.*

When the two men arrive at the altar Lymond is waiting on the steps and, allowing Gabriel to put his case first, he sits down and says 'like a crone on a creepie stool, I shall sit here and marvel.' In the days before pews or seats were provided, parishioners might bring their own stools to listen to sermons. A creepie stool or 'low stool' in Scots may have been simply such a small seat but, more aptly in this instance, the term could also be used to describe a stool in a church where offenders sat for public rebuke.

Jerott watches the confrontation between Lymond and Gabriel on and in front of the altar steps. When Gabriel is unmasked and uses the Chevalier de Seurre as a human shield, there seems to be a chance that he might escape:

*If he were quick, he might just manage to slip inside and round the altar, past the Chapel of the Holy Cross and out of the church by the Lady Steps ...*

This exit was in the far north-eastern corner, at the Virgin's niche, and lay at the end of the Holy Cross Aisle. Before Gabriel can run, however, Lymond frees de Seurre by launching himself at Gabriel from the altar rails 'like some chill, periastral missile.' As Jerott and the other witnesses move back, 'within the altar rails, on the steps, on the fine Turkey carpet before the steps, there was no one but the two men facing one another from a space of a few yards, steel in hand.' The church deacon tries to intervene just as 'more than a hundred feet above their heads, above the choir roof vaulting ... the moaning bell started to toll.' One of the three bells of St Giles', the Moaning Bell, which tolled for the dead, was made in Flanders in 1460 and inscribed 'I mourn the dead: I call the living: I disperse the thunder'. The bell tolled nightly in the 16th century to indicate curfew:

*The odour of incense ... [came] from the big stately fabric, with its high crown of groined stone, and its great bell, that had rung out the nation's grief at the disaster of Flodden; and tonight and every night, at ten o'clock, would toll its forty strokes, in warning to the citizens of Edinburgh to keep off the streets.* (DK, Pt 3, Ch 17)

The deacon is stabbed by Gabriel, who then calls upon Randy Bell. Bell emerges from 'behind the octagonal pillar to the left of the High Altar.' After a fight with Lymond in which he cannot hope to prevail, Bell falls at the feet of d'Oisel who is somewhere near the choir.

The fight between Lymond and Gabriel continues around the altar and up and down the steps. Close, ruthless fighting ensues until finally Gabriel is quelled and Lymond calls his life forfeit, detailing his crimes and the people he has betrayed. The shocking revelation about Oonagh and her child comes whilst Gabriel lies pinned to the ground with a dagger at his throat and Lymond's visible 'agony of mind' on hearing this is emphasised as the bell stops and:

*... within the church, the silence had the quality of a forest at night. Whisperings, shufflings, jostlings, rustled through the herb-laden air, warmed by many bodies, and by the tapers, hissing and guttering in their diminishing clusters before every quiet shrine.*

Despite his intention to strike, the descent of Lymond's blade is stopped at Philippa's insistence. Freed, Gabriel flees and flings the vessel used in the Eucharist at Lymond. This article is described in detail in records of the church plate of the time but did not survive the Reformation.

*The massive monstrance with its golden bells, encrusted with pearls, stood firm at his hand. Bracing his great shoulders Graham Malett lifted it, and raising it high above his head, sent it crashing over the rails to where Lymond raced at his heels, the recovered dirk in his hand.*

Gabriel makes good his escape down the now disappeared Lady Steps to the High Street. Lymond, badly injured, asks Richard to help him walk the length of the church to make his promise to his son.

*'Over there,' said Francis Crawford. 'To Lauder's chapel. Can you help me, do you think?' He got there, in the end, to the small and beautiful chapel against St Giles's south-west wall, founded, sixty years back, by Alexander Lauder of Blyth in honour of God, the Virgin Mary, and the Archangel Gabriel.*

Added to St Giles' in the early 16th century, Lauder's chapel used to form the south-western corner of the church. It was removed in the renovation of 1829, and the site now lies outside St Giles'. The likely position of the chapel lies near the bottom of a set of stone steps leading to a private entrance used by High Court judges at important services.

### 28 Parliament Square (St Giles' Kirkyard)

Parliament Square, to the south of the church and built in the 18th century, now occupies the site of the burial ground of St Giles'. Previously, the area sloped right down to the Cowgate, and Kathi walks to the Tolbooth from the Hamilton's house there.

*The quickest way to the crown of the ridge was to climb through the burial ground of St Giles', in summer as crowded with notaries and their clients as with graves. In winter, only the custom-built shelters were occupied, but the barking of dogs came from the homes of the Provost and curate of the church, and the drone of children's voices from the school. She passed Tom Swift's big house, which her uncle had often rented, and which actually stood in the kirkyard, which she had once thought peculiar.*
*... From the top, you could look down the ridge and see the Firth of Forth, a broad grey band in the distance, with the hills of Fife sprawling beyond. (Gem, Pt 4, Ch 37)*

Within the precincts of the kirkyard was the Sang School, where boys trained for the choir, the hospital and the provost's stable. Because the slope has now been built up, the route Kathi took to the Tolbooth no longer exists and the Law Courts on the south side of the square block the view down to the Cowgate. Parliament Hall, built in the 17th century, will be of interest to visitors for its soaring hammer beam roof and was purpose-built for the parliament of the time. It is now connected to the Court of Session and lawyers meet their clients there, just as they once did in the kirkyard. The door is in the south-west corner of the square and it is open to the public. Part of the square is now a car park and John Knox's grave is said to lie under space 23, indicated by a memorial plaque 'I.K. 1572'.

## 29 The Tolbooth

In Edinburgh this now-disappeared building is referred to as the Old Tolbooth. It stood at the north-west corner of St Giles' and was a building of multiple purposes. The original purpose and name was that of Bellhouse, where tolls would be paid for leasing stalls or booths, and rules applied by burgesses. In the 14th century Robert II gave the city the land to build the Tolbooth on the north side of the market square that occupied the space to the west of St Giles', so, like the Luckenbooths, it stood in the roadway. It included some booths in its lower floors, was extended over the centuries to suit the needs of the city, and ultimately reached four or five storeys in height.

The Old Tolbooth in the 19th century

A number of courts met within the Tolbooth and, whilst the function of burgh Town House remained (the Town Council meeting there for centuries and tolls continuing to be collected), it also became prison accommodation, and it was where those condemned to death awaited their fate. As the burgh evolved into the capital of Scotland the Tolbooth accommodated the Scottish Parliament.

> *On a Monday in early December, the Parliament of Scotland met in the Tolbooth of Edinburgh for the first time since March ...* (Gem*, Pt 5, Ch 47)*

In 1561 it was already in a ruinous state but continued in use until it was demolished in 1817. The site of the building is marked on the cobblestones with brass setts, and the entrance, where public executions took place, with a granite heart, after Sir Walter Scott's description of the site as the 'Heart of Midlothian' in the novel of that name. There is a continuing tradition to spit on the heart, which now is seen as lucky but perhaps reflects an earlier disdain for what the building represented or for those condemned to die there.

For Nicholas, the Tolbooth is a place where he helps to steer the nation:

> *[Gelis knew] where she would find [Nicholas]... nothing was left to the architects of the nation's affairs but to assemble ... in the Tolbooth, that strong irregular building, parliament hall, court and prison ... which had become the unofficial council chamber of Scotland.* (Gem*, Pt 5, Ch 45)*

For Lymond it is courthouse and prison:

> *Inside the Tolbooth, the sun piped in through the coloured glass of the windows. The Assize was preparing, in a narrow room above the hall where Parliament would sit tomorrow. Twelve Assessors ... sat on three sides of a long board at one end.* (GoK, Pt 4, Ch 4)

> *... [a] candle shone in an upper window at the Tolbooth: behind it Lymond lay, drugged into sleep, with a guard outside his locked door until the night should pass and Parliament meet to pronounce his doom.* (GoK, Pt 4, Ch 4)

For Kathi, the small shops provide a place for a little spying:

> *... she pushed her way ... to the Old Tolbooth, and the expensive booths rented yearly ... Mostly the same traders leased them, but after the Martinmas reshuffle, it always took time to locate everybody ... There were about thirty small chambers, some on the north side of the old public building, and some on the south. Others had been constructed underneath in the vaults, and some were tucked into landings and crammed under the stairs. There were five booths and a desirable cellar fitted into the bellhouse.* (Gem, Pt 4, Ch 37)

### 30 The Luckenbooths

First built in 1440 and demolished in 1817, the Luckenbooths, also known as the Buith Raw or Stinkand Raw, stood in the roadway of the High Street, nestling along the north wall of St Giles'. This row of irregular tenements with booths, where traders could sell their wares by day and which could be locked behind them by night, was originally two storeys high. Over subsequent centuries some reached four storeys and the row was extended westwards until it met the wall of the Tolbooth. In later centuries the roof of the westernmost Luckenbooth acted as the platform for public execution.

> *Now, cautiously, lights glimmered in the high lands above the booths and the church; shutters creaked back, and candlelight on first one high balcony, then another, glinted on the brass rail and the peering flesh of the owners, craning above.* (DK, Pt 4, Ch 17)

The Stinkand Style was a narrow dark lane that ran between the Luckenbooths and the wall of St Giles'. There, traders also set up temporary stalls called kraimes (or crames) between the buttresses of the church to sell their wares. The footprint of the buildings is marked on the pavement and road by brass setts. Heart-shaped luckenbooth brooches have long been traditional love tokens in Scotland and are still associated with Edinburgh. Many houses also had lock-up shops on their ground floor street frontage. Examples can be seen at Gladstone's Land and John Knox House.

In *The Disorderly Knights*, the Luckenbooths were scene of the murder of Wat Scott of Buccleuch. The highlighted text overleaf outlines the events of this scene.

St Giles' and the Luckenbooths, early 19th century

## Buccleuch's Death – *The Disorderly Knights* (Pt 3, Ch 17)

*... in the dirt, lay the disjointed carcass, wet, warm, grossly squandered like soft fruit, which for the better part of seventy years had answered the heroic spirit of Walter Scott of Buccleuch.*

The death of Buccleuch in the Luckenbooths is based on a real historical event that took place on 4th October 1552 as a result of the long-running feud between the Scotts and the Kerrs. Dorothy Dunnett paints a vivid picture of the murder and these long-gone buildings. Here is a guide for those wanting to imagine the event.

The Kerrs arrive in Edinburgh believing that Buccleuch is going to expose the fraud they had perpetrated with George Paris. From the West Bow, Cessford and Hume walk to Buccleuch's house next to the Salt Tron towards the bottom of the High Street.

*[They] passed from the wide market into the narrow channel of the Queen's High Street ... choked by the straggling line of locked timber shops, the Booth Raw, down*

*its middle. There they took the foot passage, narrow and dark, on the right of the Luckenbooths, where the tall bulk of the Tolbooth ... loomed dark in the night ... And next to it, as they passed, a lamp hung in the Norman porch of the great church of St Giles ... [they] reached the east end of the Stinkand Style, past the booths and church, and were in the open High Street, with the Mercat Cross on their left, and on their right the entrance to Conn's Close.*

They receive news of Paris's capture just as they reach the empty house and know they are too late to hide their wrongdoing ... 'but there was time for vengeance: all the time in the world.' They leave Robert Kerr at the house and retrace their steps back towards St Giles'.

Meanwhile, Buccleuch is on his way home, leaving Paris imprisoned in the Tolbooth 'round the graveyard at the back of St Giles', which he rounded at Our Lady's Steps on his way to walk down to his lodging '... a dark shadow trudging past the pale grey bulk of the church.'

He meets Cessford and Hume at the north-east corner of the church, next to the Lady Steps lit by 'feeble light from the Virgin's statue in its niche above the church's north-east doorway' where a violent confrontation ensues that ends with a mortally injured Buccleuch hidden in one of the locked booths, 'his blood ebbing fast with his life.' The niche that lit the scene lay at the north-east corner of St Giles', above eye level, but the statue of the Virgin was removed at the time of the Reformation.

Cessford and Hume make their escape down Conn's Close. Half an hour later Robert Kerr enters the Luckenbooths hearing 'the low whining breath that might be a dog's, but which proved to be the high heart of Buccleuch' and finishes the job with his sword. Although he and his companions slip down Conn's Close he manages to alert Macullo, Bute Herald, who calls out to them: 'the light from [Bute Herald's] bearer's lantern fell ... on the men who, emerging from the Booth Raw, slipped quickly downstreet to Conn's Close.'

Lymond and Jerott have by now begun to search for Buccleuch, who they know is in mortal danger. Also arriving at the West Bow they pass the Luckenbooth, heading for Buccleuch's house. Hearing the noise of Macullo's challenge, they return and find the old man, newly dead 'behind the broken-hinged door of a booth, with the reek of decayed food and animals thick in the darkness.' Moments later Gabriel arrives on the scene, calls for Lymond's arrest and 'suddenly, with a hiss of drawn steel, the trampling feet of an army seemed to converge on Lymond' who escapes 'striking through the rotten back of the booth ... into the jostling darkness beyond', making his way to St Giles' to claim sanctuary, with Jerott delaying pursuit for a few vital moments.

The arrival of law officers allows Jerott to escape Gabriel's dagger and while the monks of the Maison Dieu are being summoned 'to carry the heavy, disfigured body into their quiet chapel.' Jerott realises that he and Gabriel

*... were being carried past both Stinkand Raw, church and Tolbooth, and that the*

*crowd, swirling round the west corner of the tall prison, had debouched along the graveyard path beyond, spilling among the grey tombstones ... among the grey buttresses of the side and back of St Giles [until they reached] the wide steps leading up to the south porch of the church.*

Buccleuch's death did not prevent the Scotts' continuing importance in the ensuing centuries. In the square at the west door of St Giles' stands the statue of the Fifth Duke of Buccleuch, a distant descendant of Wat and Will Scott.

### 31 Mercat Cross

The Mercat Cross has stood in its current position since the 19th century only. It stood in the middle of the High Street from 1365 until it was removed in 1756 when the thoroughfare was widened. The Cross was mostly destroyed, but some detailed descriptions remain.

A tall pillar decorated with thistles and medallions and topped with a unicorn, the cross provided a platform for proclamations including the naming of those unfortunate enough to be put to the horn (outlawed) as Lymond is in *The Game of Kings*. It was also a place of public punishment and execution, particularly for the crime of treason, as well as a focus for trade. The 1617 location is marked in the

The Mercat Cross

road opposite Fleshmarket Close. In the 15th and 16th centuries it had been a few yards east of this and its position in the thoroughfare explains why the cross was on their left as the Kerrs passed down the hill to Buccleuch's house.

The only piece of the original is the central pillar, which, because of the damage done in the 18th century, is several feet the shorter than formerly but has been topped once more by a unicorn.

### 32 Conn's Close

This close no longer exists but ran from the High Street down to the Cowgate in the locality of the private Burnet's and Covenant Closes. It was named for John Con [*sic*], a flesher, and demolished at some point in the 18th century. It appears in the scene of Buccleuch's death.

### 33 Bell's Wynd (Maison Dieu)

At the head of this close in the 16th century lay a hospital or almshouse named *Maison Dieu* where monks tended those in need. In *The Disorderly Knights* Buccleuch's body is taken to rest there after he is murdered.

*[The Watch] ... summoned the monks from the Maison Dieu at the head of Bell's Wynd to carry the heavy, disfigured body into their quiet chapel.* (DK, Pt 3, Ch 17)

### 34 Tron Kirk (Buccleuch's house)
This Kirk, no longer in use as a church, was built at the site of the Salt Tron, a weighing arm used to measure goods. In an excavated area beneath the floor lies part of an old close called Marlin's Wynd. Buccleuch's house is in this area, as described in *The Disorderly Knights*.

*Below [Conn's Close] on their right was the Tron, and beside it the tall house with its corbelled oriels, the slatted flats rising crooked above their heads, where Buccleuch had his lodging.* (DK, Pt 3, Ch 17)

## E Upper High Street – North Side

### 35 ADVOCATE'S CLOSE
This picturesque and steep stairway gives a particularly good impression of the High Street's position on a precipice and is a good example of the kind of closes that Nicholas and Julius tumble in and out of when, towards the end of *Gemini*, they have their fist fight after leaving the Kilmirren house in Castlehill.

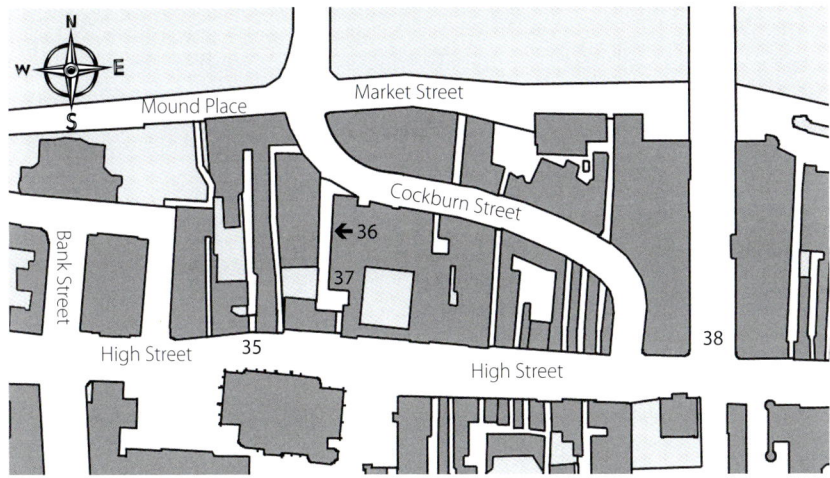

### E UPPER HIGH STREET – NORTH SIDE
35  Advocate's Close
36  Warriston's Close (Bruce's Close/Culter house)
37  Mary King's Close
38  North Bridge (Halkerston's Wynd)

> *And it was as crazy a ruffle as anyone would ettle to see, with the pair of them rolling and staggering and ducking and swinging from the Butter Tron down to St Giles, up and down steps, into and out of closes ... rolling down, down, down until they came to the steepest vennel that led to the Nor' Loch, and tumbled down that, fighting still ...* (Gem, Pt 4, Ch 42)

### 36 Warriston's Close (Bruce's Close)

As previously described, the Culter house was both in the High Street and Bruce's Close.

> *The Culters house in Bruce's Close had a red roof and a motto over every window; but inside it was comfortable and convenient, with two separate bedrooms and a parlour with a wide, light window above the garden for Sybilla's sewing.* (GoK, Pt 4, Ch 4)

Warriston's Close is next to the City Chambers. The area has been remodelled extensively over the centuries and the original entrance has been built over, but the close can be accessed from Writers' Court where the entrance to the attraction 'The Real Mary King's Close' also lies. The close has been foreshortened by the building of Cockburn Street further down the slope.

It was previously known as Bruce's Close so this is possibly the site of the Culter residence. The names of closes changed over time in accordance with important residents, and Robert Bruce of Binnie built or extended a house there in the 16th century. A lintel of that house remains, on the west side of the close, inscribed '*Gratia Dei Robertus Bruis*'. Whilst we can't know for certain that Dorothy Dunnett had this close in mind, the fact that her work is highly researched and usually historically accurate indicates that she would likely have used a completely fictitious name if she had intended it to be elsewhere on the High Street. The views from Sybilla's window locate it firmly on the north side of the High Street. There is, however, no red-roofed house with mottoes over the windows to guide us, so the location of the fictional house is speculative. John Knox lived in Warriston's Close during much of his time in Edinburgh, which would have made him a close neighbour of the Culters in Bruce's Close.

While Sybilla waits in Edinburgh for Lymond's trial, she looks out over her garden. To capture a similar view today, it's best to take a vantage point from the upper reaches of either Warriston's or Advocate's Close. The locations she sees appear in the map 'Edinburgh, Canongate and Surrounding Villages' on p. 4.

> *Sybilla looked out of the dark window. To the east, Moultrie's Hill and the Dow Craig, with Greenside on its farther slopes; where for nine hours she had once sat and watched Davie Lindsay mock the Three Estates before the Three Estates, and the Crown before the Crown.* (GoK, Pt 4, Ch 4)

Moultrie's Hill is much less obviously a hill now, as it lies at the area at the end of North Bridge as it meets Princes Street. The Dow Craig is an alternative name for Calton Hill, which rises to your right, with the distinctive monuments balanced on its peak. Greenside lies near the north-western slope of Calton Hill and was used for archery, arms practice and the occasional theatrical performance as, for example, Sybilla's remembered first performance in Edinburgh of *Ane Pleasant Satyre of the Thrie Estaitis*, a satirical morality play in Middle Scots, written by Sir David Lyndsay:

> *The Lang Gait and Gabriel's road, unlit; and few and distant lights from Broughton and Silver Mills and Kirkbraehead and Canon Mills. Below, her garden plunged and rolled to the turgid waters of the loch, and the tall lands on either side shifted their shadows with the shifting moon.* (GoK, Pt 4, Ch 4)

The Lang Gait, or Lang Dyke, was a road on the other side of the Nor' Loch that followed roughly the route of today's Princes Street. Gabriel's Road ran behind it to the north-west. Broughton, Silvermills, Kirkbraehead and Canonmills are all areas of Edinburgh that were once villages and are now part of the modern city.

The house makes an appearance in The House of Niccolò. When Nicholas continues to meet people after arriving at the top of the West Bow on his way from the Grassmarket to Kilmirren House, he has a tantalising glimpse of a house strikingly similar to Sybilla's:

> *He was at the top of the Bow. [He spoke] ... to the priest of St Giles' whom he had to turn downhill to meet. ... [He] was watching the street. Most of the houses were known to him now. There was a handsome one opposite, with a red roof and mottoes.* (UH, Pt 1, Ch 5)

This is surely a description of the same house, although there are challenges in pinpointing the location. This text appears, at first sight, to suggest the house being nearer the Lawnmarket. However, Nicholas's walk down to speak to the priest could put him very near this location, which is opposite St Giles' on the High Street. The writer's view is that this description is of the Culter house in Bruce's Close, but the reader may wish to draw their own conclusions.

---

**37 MARY KING'S CLOSE**

The Real Mary King's Close attraction explores a part of underground Edinburgh. Before the 19th century this area comprised Mary King's Close, Stewart's Close, Pearson's Close, Allan's Close and Craig's Close but the upper portions were demolished to make way for the City Chambers in1753. The lower parts of the closes, however, have remained. The tours, even though led somewhat theatrically by costumed guides, do give a fascinating insight into life within the closes. They give you the chance to explore a part of Edinburgh that is rarely seen and has not had the extensive remodelling of buildings above ground.

Down here it is not too hard to imagine Edinburgh busy and overcrowded, with people of wealth and abject poverty living on top of one another. It also demonstrates the narrow closes that Nicholas and Julius fought through without the modern niceties of steps for the steeper hills. That neither of them suffered a broken neck in the process is perhaps more by good luck than good judgement:

> And it was then, as he got up, that you could see that the big man, bless my soul, was Nicol de Fleury, his face covered in bruises, and the man he was attacking was the lawyer fellow. (Gem, Pt 4, Ch 42)

### 38 North Bridge (Halkerston's Wynd)

North Bridge meets the High Street just downhill from the Tron Kirk. It crosses the valley to Moultrie's Hill, once visible from Sybilla's window. Halkerston's Wynd ran below what is now the eastern pavement on North Bridge, descending into the valley to the Physic Garden of the Church of the Trinity.

On an occasion when Nicholas doesn't want to go to the Trinity Church:

> [Will Roger] let the renewed struggle run its course which it duly did, ending near the top of Halkerston's Wynd with four men shackling Nicholas by the arms and another hitched in immobilising fashion on his back. Halkerston's Wynd led to the church of the Trinity. Will Roger said, '– or we could roll you down. Yes or no?' (TLWL, Pt 2, Ch 14)

New Port was built at the foot of Halkerston's Wynd in the 16th century adding to the defences of Edinburgh on the route to Leith. The roadway and western pavement of North Bridge now stand above where, at the bottom of the valley, lay the sluices for the Nor' Loch.

## F Lower High Street

### 39 Blackfriars Street (Blackfriars Wynd)

Blackfriars Wynd led to the Dominican monastery, which was on the farther side of the Cowgate. Both David de Salmeton and Prosper de Camulio stayed in the guestrooms there in *Gemini*.

> At just over fifty, he had begun to weather, in the way that run-about envoys usually did, whether representing a Duke or a Pope. Nevertheless, his black eyes beamed upon Nicholas, entering his comfortable guest-room in the monastery of the Dominicans, Edinburgh. Nicholas, who had never minded Prosper de Camulio, beamed back. He said, 'I like the robes.' (Gem, Pt 1, Ch 7)

### 40 Chalmers Close (Trinity Apse)

All that remains of the Church of the Trinity, which features in *To Lie With Lions*, is the apse, which was rebuilt here in Chalmers Close in the 19th century.

It is the building with the arched windows on the right, part way down the stairs, and is still owned by Edinburgh City Council.

In 1848 the church was scheduled to be pulled down but such was the public outcry at the demolition of so important a medieval church that it was dismantled instead, stored on Calton Hill and the pieces numbered for future reconstruction. Thirty years

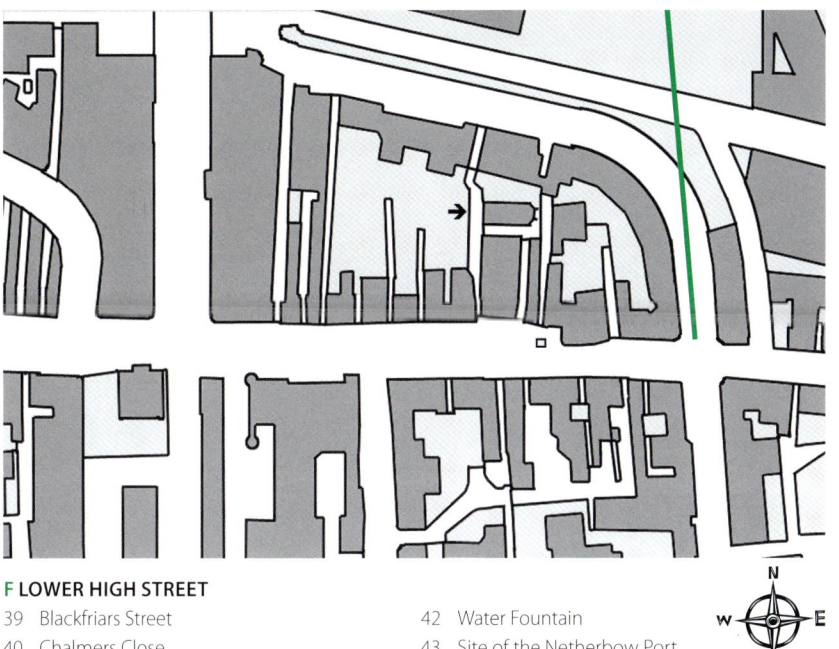

### F LOWER HIGH STREET
39  Blackfriars Street
40  Chalmers Close
41  John Knox House
42  Water Fountain
43  Site of the Netherbow Port
━  Original route of Leith Wynd

and numerous arguments passed before the church could be rebuilt on its current site, but many of the numbered stones had been stolen for other buildings and it was possible to rebuild only the apse.

The Church of the Trinity was a collegiate church built by Mary of Guelders in 1460 in memory of her husband, James II, who was killed by the exploding cannon that makes a brief and rather wet appearance at the start of *Niccolò Rising*. The church was dedicated to the Holy Trinity, the Blessed Virgin, St Ninian and All Saints and stood at the foot of Leith Wynd at the eastern end of Nor' Loch where Waverley Station is now.

**The Church of the Trinity in the 19th century**

*There was a virtue in simplicity. Here, the beauty lay in the strictness of the lines and the delicacy of the colour, complementing each other, so that the proportion of the whole was deeply pleasing: an imposing ninety feet from the bright cup of the apse to the rood tower behind him. (TLWL, Pt 2, Ch 14)*

The lands associated with the church included a manse, Trinity Hospital and the Physic Garden, which Clémence mentions when the loch freezes in *To Lie With Lions*. In Nicholas's time it would have been a relatively new building, and was a particularly beautiful example of Gothic medieval architecture.

**Interior of the Church of the Trinity in the 19th century**

*Silent; cool as a forest the pillars receded, seemingly empty, leading the eye to the east, where a single lamp hung above a group of gowned men round a lectern ... The tiles were glazed. They glimmered green and yellow and brown, double-netted like fish where the window-leads caught them ... The coloured designs on the windows hugged the shafts of the piers like embroidery on an Angevin doublet, in and out of the pleats, teasing up to the floriate collar of the capitals, which promptly exploded in clamour. The stone pealed. The capitals became the surrogate mouths of the organ. (*TLWL*, Pt 2, Ch 14)*

Also in *To Lie With Lions* the church is hired out for Will Roger to rehearse the musicians for the Nativity Play, which enables its Provost, John Bonkle's father, to commission Hugo vander Goes to paint the altarpiece that appears in *Gemini*.

*The collegiate church of the Trinity, which had filled its coffers by renting itself out as a music-room, made known its loyal desire to commission a triptych depicting the monarch, his Queen, and Edward Bonkle, the Provost of Trinity. The initial response, such as it was, indicated that a donation in cash might be preferable.* (TLWL, Pt 2, Ch 19)

The surviving panels are on display in the National Gallery, and the church plate and original stonework in the Museum of Scotland.

### 41 JOHN KNOX HOUSE AND MOUBRAY HOUSE

These two buildings, or parts of them, would have been known by both Nicholas and Lymond.

John Knox House, reputed to be the last dwelling place of the Protestant reformer, is owned by the Church of Scotland but also linked to the Scottish Storytelling Centre, and is now run as a museum telling the story of John Knox. Described as 'improbably picturesque', it remains one of the oldest houses in Edinburgh, and is notable for its external stair, overhanging upper floors and crow step gable end. Parts of the building date back to 1470, and it lies near the site of the Netherbow. John Knox never appears in the books, although he is mentioned in *Checkmate* when Lymond is cared for after his collapse in Dieppe. He became a powerful figure in the Scottish Reformation and he was frequently at odds with Mary, Queen of Scots. Knox also lived in Warriston's Close.

Previously, the house was owned by the Mossman family, who were jewellers to the royal family of Scotland. Sir John refashioned earlier material into the Crown of Scotland in 1540 for James V. He survived the battle of Solway Moss and was the father of Sir James Mossman, who was jeweller and goldsmith to Mary, Queen of Scots.

The house extends over three floors, with a stone turnpike staircase, painted ceilings and oak panelling. It gives a good impression of a house of the 16th century, including the layout of luckenbooths, on the ground floor and includes furniture gleaned from other Royal Mile houses.

Moubray House lies next door to John Knox House, and although the facade is early 17th century, gives a good impression of a typical Edinburgh tenement from Nicholas's and Lymond's day. It was built for Andrew Moubray, burgess, in 1477 and further extended in 1530 by his son. The frontage has been restored, with timber jetties and an external stair to reflect the original building, which would also have had luckenbooths on the ground floor. It is not open to the public.

#### 42 WATER FOUNTAIN

On the pavement next to John Knox House is one of the original ten city water fountains. They ran with wine to celebrate special occasions and on one notable night at the start of *The Game of Kings*:

*Mungo need not have worried. The lower cellar, the cavern and the long underground tunnel to the Nor' Loch contained no contraband at all. But, because tuns of Bordeaux wine make hard rowing, all the wells of Edinburgh ran with claret next day; and on this, the eve of the English invasion, the commonality of the High Street were for an hour or two as blithe as the Gosford Close sow.* (GoK, Opening Gambit)

### 43 The Netherbow Port

The site of the Netherbow Port is marked with brass plates on the cobbles at the crossroads with St Mary's Street and Jeffrey Street, and a plaque on the wall on the north side of the High Street. In both the King's and Flodden Walls the Netherbow was the largest and most fortified gate. It led to the Canongate, marked the division between the two burghs and allowed traffic from Leith and the sea into Edinburgh. It appears in both series, and is very close to Ca' Niccolò, which lay in the Canongate. Taxes would be paid at this old gate in the wall and the heads of executed criminals displayed to deter those thinking of misdeeds. It is possible that this is the fate that awaited Lymond at the end of *The Game of Kings* had not Will Scott shown such a talent for tarocco.

Nicholas passes through it many times on the way to and from his Canongate house, and it can be seen from the top floor.

49

*Twice [Gelis] climbed to the top of the house and stood on the balcony that looked uphill towards the Netherbow Gate and the buildings of Edinburgh. (TLWL, Pt 2, Ch 11)*

It was demolished in 1764 to make the thoroughfare more passable to traffic.

The Netherbow Port from the Canongate, 18th century

## G Canongate

Edinburgh's neighbouring burgh does not feature in The Lymond Chronicles at all, but important characters in The House of Niccolò have properties there of which Dorothy Dunnett specifies the location of only two.

Describing the location of his Canongate house and referring both to Bruges and the incident at Hesdin, Nicholas says to Gelis:

*You remember the Canongate? Like Spangnaerts Street sloped like a chute, with Holyrood Abbey in place of the mattresses. (TLWL, Pt 1, Ch 8)*

Immediately outside the Netherbow, St Mary's Wynd ran to the south and Leith Wynd to the north, alongside the wall.

### 44 St Mary's Street (St Mary's Wynd)

St Mary's Wynd lay just below the Netherbow, around the current site of St Mary's Street opposite Leith Wynd and Nicholas's Canongate house. It was named for a convent and hospital, which lay just outside the city wall and was renamed in the 19th century. It descended to the Cowgate and St Mary's Port was near its southern end. As the road crossed the valley, the Cowgate Port pierced the Flodden Wall to the right. This was the main south gate and big enough for livestock to be driven along the road to the Grassmarket. The Kerrs' messenger leaves through this gate to inform d'Oisel of Wat Scott's death, and d'Oisel and Gabriel enter the city through St Mary's Port, ride up St Mary's Wynd and through the Netherbow:

*... a boy, well bribed in advance, left the Cowgate Port ... and riding round to the south-east came across [d'Oisel's] night encampment, just outside the wall ... Five minutes later, Sir Graham at his own request by his side, d'Oisel was riding fast through St Mary's Port and up to the High Street ... (DK, Pt 3, Ch 17)*

### 45 The Flodden Wall

St Mary's Street now continues as the Pleasance as it goes up the hill beyond. Looking down the road you can see that as it begins to ascend the hill it is bordered by a thick wall of pale stone on the right. This is the largest surviving piece of the Flodden Wall and once enclosed Blackfriars Monastery, which has long since disappeared.

## 46 Jeffrey Street (Leith Wynd)

Although this area has been much remodelled over the years, the head of Leith Wynd used to lie where the top of Jeffrey Street is now. It was a straight road that led towards Leith from Edinburgh and the Canongate. It ran down the slope alongside the wall just beyond the Netherbow so it had houses on only one side. The wynd ran past the Collegiate Church of the Trinity then led to the Wester Road to Leith:

> *In Scotland, it pleased Nicholas de Fleury to make his public entry into the King's town of Edinburgh in a royal cavalcade, passing up the incline of Leith Wynd, and turning his back on the house of Archie of Berecrofts and Anselm Sersanders in order to pass through the portals that led to the High Street.* (Gem, Pt 1, Ch 3)

## 47 Ca' Niccolò

The bank's headquarters is built on Berecrofts land, next to the Berecrofts' family house, when Nicholas first arrives in Edinburgh:

> *'Master Nicholas has got some good competent ground, and is building himself a stone house in the Canongate.'* (UH, Pt 1, Ch 2)

The business is based there, and although he sells the house back to Archie Berecrofts at one point, he regains it by the end of *Gemini*. It is referred to by a number of different names including the Edinburgh headquarters of the Banco di Niccolò, Ca' Niccolò, Floory Land and Tigh a' Nichol (House of Nichol). It has side windows looking onto Leith Wynd, so must have been the first house outside the gates of the Netherbow where the corner house on the east side of Jeffrey Street now is. Strategically, for links to Edinburgh and the world beyond via the port of Leith, there can have been no more convenient spot for Nicholas's business.

Its position is described in the description of the Entry of Margaret of Denmark:

> *The Canongate was draped with scarlet for the Entry of Margaret of Denmark, and the houses lining Leith Wynd hung arras and cloths from their sills ... In the Banco di Niccolò the upper loggia creaked with the number of neighbours and guests who packed into it ... Gregorio left his task as joint host and climbed the staircase to the small casement window which gave on to Leith Wynd.* (UH, Pt 1, Ch 21)

Although unaware of Nicholas's plan to ruin Scotland and the role the house would play, when he first sees it:

> *Gregorio experienced fear. In spite of all that Julius had said, he had not been prepared for the reality: for the tall, secretive house in the Canongate which Nicholas had fitted into the enclave of ecclesiastics and merchants and from which his business was run.* (UH, Pt 1, Ch 18)

A little later Dorothy Dunnett affords us a comparison with Sybilla's panorama:

## G CANONGATE

44  St Mary's Street (St Mary's Wynd)
45  The Flodden Wall
46  Jeffrey Street (Leith Wynd)
47  Site of Ca' Niccolò
48  Site of the Berecrofts House
49  Site of Kathi and Robin's, and Tobie's Houses
50  St John Street
51  Canongate Tolbooth
52  Museum of Edinburgh
53  Canongate Kirk
54  Dunbar's Close
—  Original route of Leith Wynd

*It was not a short view, such as you got from a window in Bruges. Behind the Canongate houses, the open land bumped its way past leekbeds and pastures and fruit trees to a narrow valley, and then rose beyond to a fine sunlit crag grazed by sheep. Immediately below, the paved back yards of this house and its neighbours were crammed with a jumble of stables and wells, bakehouses and byres, styes and henhouses and sheds. Into this space, admitted by the vaulted passage that led from*

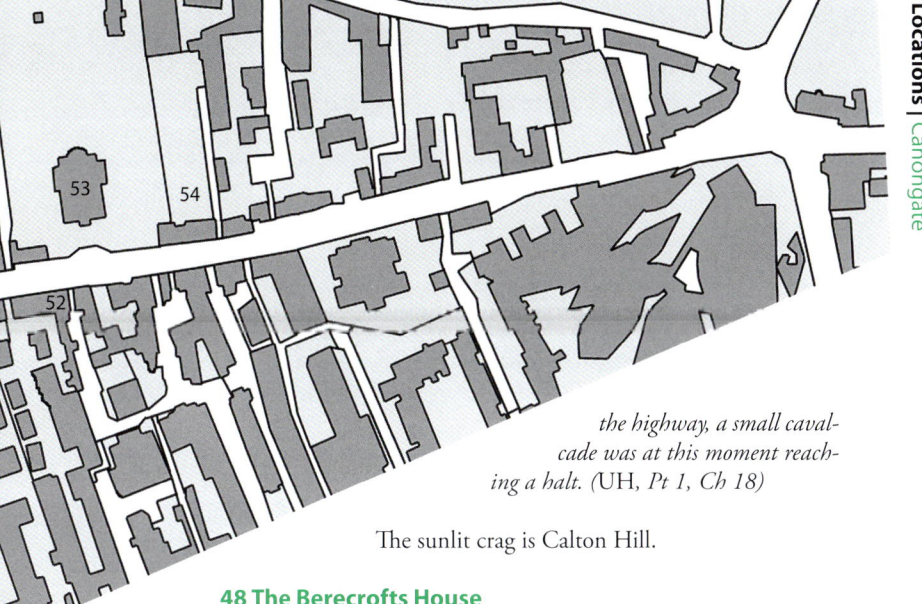

*the highway, a small cavalcade was at this moment reaching a halt.* (UH, Pt 1, Ch 18)

The sunlit crag is Calton Hill.

### 48 The Berecrofts House

The home of Archie Berecrofts is next door to Nicholas's so must have been slightly further down the Canongate.
A spy reporting to Nicholas and Julius passes through the Netherbow:

> On his left was the road that plunged downhill and northwards to Leith. Ahead was the highway to Holyrood Abbey. Packed between the two was the merchant colony presided over by the family Berecrofts, among which was the house of the Banco di Niccolò ... (UH, Pt 1, Ch 4)

There was a passage, which might have been called a 'trance', between the two houses and their business and fortunes were likewise linked.

> ... [Gelis] heard the cavalcade as it swept under her window from Leith Wynd, and even heard the crash of Berecrofts's door as it was flung open. Then it was upon her own door that someone was hammering. Archie Berecrofts stood outside ... (TLWL, Pt 4, Ch 30)

And later:

> These days, the connecting door to the Berecrofts house stood permanently open. (Gem, Pt 5, Ch 49)

### 49 Kathi and Robin's and Tobie's Houses

When Robin returns to Scotland with Kathi after his injury, they take a house on the opposite side of the Canongate from Nicholas and Archie Berecrofts, presumably very

53

near the head of St Mary's Wynd:

> *[Archie said] I've been thinking. There's a house over the way. They could have that. We'd widen the doors for lifting him out and the same over here. (Gem, Pt 1, Ch 7)*

Tobie and Clémence also made their home in the Canongate, in the same complex as Robin and Kathi, but separate enough that Johndie Mar could be accommodated there in secret:

> *Over the road, Robin's father, in his level way, had resumed business ... In [Robin and Kathi's] own house, the children had settled with Cristen, and Dr Tobie and Clémence had made a home of their building in the same yard. Robin was mobile now, wheeled from one room to another, and often over the road to Saunders's office. It had once belonged to Nicholas, and had its own door. (Gem, Pt 1, Ch 10)*

Tobie's medical practice, though, is pursued from the Argyll inn, which is also used by Nicholas for private meetings:

> *Some physicians, preferring not to lodge in a great household, operated from their homes. Most followed the custom of Bruges and rented rooms in a tavern, which were also used by other professionals, such as scribes or lawyers or notaries. Himself, he liked the Argyll inn, because he admired the great Campbell who owned it ... Argyll's tavern made just the kind of meeting-place Nicholas wanted, when he needed John or Andro or Tobie to tell him what was happening, or to meet Colin Campbell himself, or Scheves or Whitelaw or Avandale outside their houses. (Gem, Pt 2, Ch 17)*

Although Dorothy Dunnett does not indicate the location of the inn, there were and remain a plethora of drinking establishments in the High Street.

#### 50 ST JOHN'S STREET AND CROSS
St John's Pend leads to St John's Street. The Order of the Knights Hospitaller of St John owned property in this area on land that belonged to neither Edinburgh nor Canongate. Just uphill from the pend a Maltese Cross is marked in the cobbles with a plaque, which marks the original position of the standing Cross of St John. The steps of this boundary cross between the Canongate and Edinburgh became a traditional meeting place and were used for public proclamations.

#### 51 CANONGATE TOLBOOTH
Although later (it dates from 1592), the Canongate Tolbooth, which now houses the People's Story (a social history museum), still looks like the tollhouse, council chamber, court and prison it once was with its bell tower and outside stair.

#### 52 MUSEUM OF EDINBURGH
The Museum of Edinburgh is situated on either side of Bakehouse Close. The buildings

Canongate Kirk

date from the 16th and 17th centuries and were subdivided in the 19th century to accommodate over three hundred people. Although later named Huntly House, the building was once called the Speaking House, because of the Latin inscriptions on the exterior walls that date back to the mid-16th century. For example:

*VT TV LINGVAE SIC EGO MEAR(VM) AVRIM(M) DOMINVS SVM* – *As thou art (master) of my tongue, so I am master of my ears.*

The building illustrates the layout of a typical land of the Canongate, with a close leading to an open courtyard. Refurbished in 2012, the facade is now painted in ochre and red, not unusual in the heyday of the Renaissance. Its focus is the history of Edinburgh and Leith from early times to the present day, and views major events through the eyes of its citizens with exhibits illustrating their lives. A model of the Old Town allows the reader to enjoy trying to spot the houses and haunts of Dorothy Dunnett's protagonists.

### 53 CANONGATE KIRK

This beautiful church is 17th century in origin and replaced the Abbey of Holyrood as the parish church for the Canongate. To the front is the Canongate Burgh Cross or market cross, which was moved from its original site in the middle of the road. The kirkyard beyond holds a number of famous memorials; the most relevant to the 16th century is the grave of Rizzio, Mary, Queen of Scots' secretary.

The funeral of Dorothy Dunnett's husband, Sir Alastair Dunnett, 'the inspiration of the legend of Francis Crawford, and whose love of Scotland, in word and deed, has done more for her than Lymond ever could', was held here in 1991. In 2001, her own funeral was held here.

### 54 DUNBAR'S CLOSE

A few steps through the archway lies a hidden gem of the Old Town. The close leads to a small park which has been laid out in the style and character of a 17th-century garden and is open to the public during daylight hours. There are still hidden gardens in the Old Town, which recall the lands that once lay behind the main street. It is not so difficult to imagine Sybilla's garden in this scented haven from the bustle of the city although, this far down the hill, the incline is gentler than the fictional land of the Culters' house.

The Palace of Holyroodhouse

## Holyrood

Holyrood Abbey and the Palace of Holyroodhouse stand side by side at the foot of the Canongate on a portion of the street called Abbey Strand from where the Abbey is to the left (north) of the Palace. You can only visit the Abbey after your tour of the Palace but before you go in to buy your ticket you might want to make a preliminary investigation of the location of Nicholas's Nativity Play. A full explanation of the importance of this is given in the highlighted text. For now, stand in the road to the left of today's entrance to the Palace to find a unicorn plaque that marks the position of the original gatehouse of the Abbey. Brass letters 'S' are marked in the pavement on Abbey Strand to indicate the extent of religious sanctuary associated with the Abbey. This area was used by those claiming sanctuary to escape debts.

The Abbey pre-dates the Palace by some four hundred years but the monarchs of medieval Scotland enjoyed life in the buildings around the Abbey; buildings which eventually grew from guest chambers to royal lodgings to a royal palace that remains in regular use by the current royal family as their residence in Edinburgh. Holyrood was less exposed to the elements than the older Edinburgh Castle and was enhanced by nearby hunting.

> *The dust here in Holyroodhouse came from the rebuilding of the royal household's lodgings, which they so often preferred to the windy fort on the ridge-top ... Everyone in Scotland seemed to have building-fever. Construction men travelled from palace to palace in jolly companies, like some new, free-drinking monastic order.* (Gem, Pt 2, Ch 2)

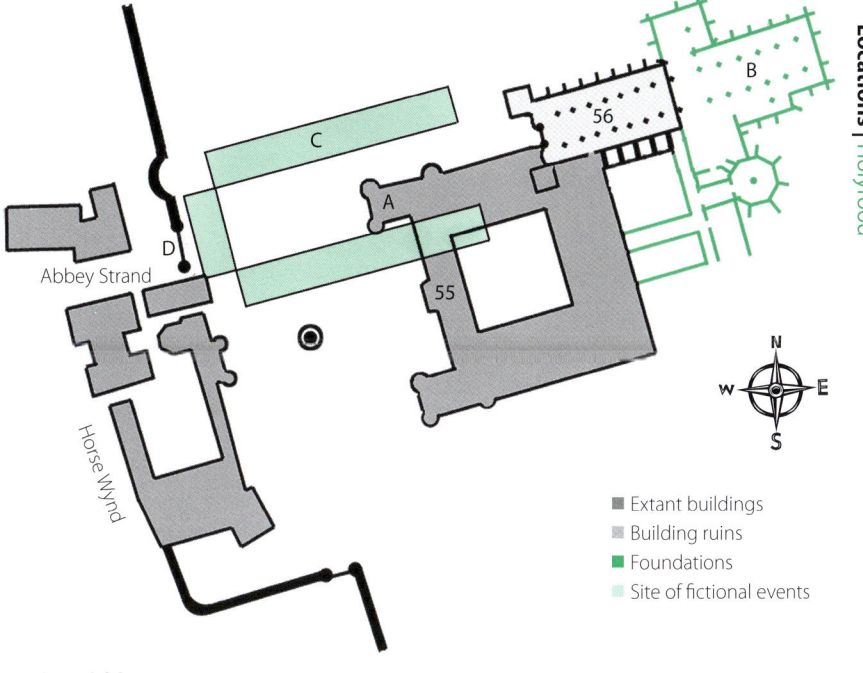

#### H **HOLYROOD**
55 Palace of Holyroodhouse
A James V's Tower
56 Ruins of Abbey Church (nave)

B Foundations of Abbey
C Site of the stands for the Nativity
D Site of Abbey Porch

The guest quarters were on the south side of the Abbey, and grew into the royal lodgings where the earliest part of the Palace stands today.

### 55 The Palace
The oldest part of the Palace is the north-west tower begun by James IV and completed by his son James V, to whom it is most often accredited. A rectangular building with round turrets on each corner, built in traditional style with security originally provided by a drawbridge and moat, it is still in use and is now attached to the rest of the Palace. The tower is mirrored by a later addition on the south side of the Palace.

Visitors are guided through the newer parts of the Palace first. Although there is little here to remind us of the Palace in Lymond's day, there are tantalising glimpses of the Renaissance in 16th-century Scotland in the Italian frescoes decorating the Grand Stair and the tapestries in the Morning Drawing Room.

The tour continues into the historic apartments in James V's Tower and for anyone interested in Scottish history, they have much to offer. Although some remodelling took place during the reign of Charles II, these rooms have a smaller, more intimate air and are more constrained in their design by thick 16th-century walls. They have an association with Mary, Queen of Scots, who used them after her return to Scotland, as did her second husband, Lord Darnley. The Outer Chamber now houses displays of Stuart and Jacobite objects. A display about Mary, Queen of Scots includes embroidered panels, a French Ordinance, crucifix, a pomander and letter. Of particular interest to Dorothy Dunnett readers is the Darnley Jewel, which belonged to Margaret Douglas, Countess of Lennox, and has a case all of its own. It is an ornate piece, heart shaped with emblems and symbols, made with enamels, rubies, blue glass and emeralds.

It is also worth looking at the Holyrood Ordinal, a liturgical manuscript dating from the mid-15th century, which detailed the rules of service for Holyrood Abbey. It sits beneath a stained glass window of St Margaret. In the 16th century this window would have looked directly down onto the Abbey.

### 56 The Abbey

Both Abbey and Palace appeared distinctly the worse for wear by the time Lymond returned to Scotland in 1547 as a result of the continuing predation of the Earl of Hertford, later Duke of Somerset and Lord Protector, in pursuance of the Rough Wooing.

Abbey Ruins

*The burned thatch, the ruined stonework, the blackened face of Holyrood Palace showed where already, in other years, invading armies from England had made their point, but not their capture.* (GoK, Opening Gambit)

Weddings were celebrated at the Abbey, including that of James III to Margaret of Denmark in *The Unicorn Hunt* and, probably, Agnes Herries and John Maxwell, whose wedding reception was clearly held in the Palace:

*Prinked and painted and stencilled with spring sunlight, the city of Edinburgh celebrated the wedding of the Lady Herries and John, Master of Maxwell, and the sound of its bells ploughed the fields of Linlithgow nearly deep enough for the barley, and made the coals quake underground at Tranent.*
*Inside the palace of Holyrood, the scene seized the eye with light and flowers, cloth of gold and bunting, and a sparkling multitude, their rents and pensions glittering on their sturdy backs* (GoK, Pt 3, Ch 3)

Numerous royal burials took place here, with those most relevant to the books being James II (following the cannon explosion at Roxburgh), James V (in the days after Solway Moss) and Mary of Guelders (after her body was moved from the Church of the Trinity), although none are described in the books.

The Abbey was abandoned as a monastic house during the Reformation and the choir and transepts demolished in 1570. Foundations of these remain to the east of the church ruins. It housed the Scottish coronation of Charles II and was converted to a Catholic Chapel Royal during the reign of James VII and II. The roof eventually collapsed in 1758, leaving it a picturesque ruin. Today only the nave of the church, open to the elements, remains. The arcades of arches and tracery, however, are still lovely and the place still has the hushed atmosphere of a church.

Nicholas's magnificent Nativity Play in *To Lie With Lions* is staged outside in the yard between the west end of the Abbey and its main gatehouse.

Visitors have an opportunity to explore the gardens, which afford some stunning views of the Abbey and Palace. In the 16th century there were enclosed gardens, as well as areas for jousting, archery, a menagerie and a tennis court, with hunting in the park beyond.

### The Nativity Play – *To Lie With Lions* (Pt 2, Ch 17 and 18)
Readers may enjoy trying to reconstruct the setting in their imaginations.

*... the inhabitants [of Edinburgh] tumbled down to the foot of the Canongate and flushed up the mountain behind, as if the ridge were indeed the chute that Nicholas once had called it.*

The 'mountain' refers to Arthur's Seat, the hill at the centre of the parkland next to Holyrood.

*Archibald, Abbot of Holyrood, was happy because he was an able, energetic man who didn't mind his entire yard being dug up and remade to hold a long rectangular platform with a stand of seats on two sides, and an end which was fixed to the porch of the Abbey. Beneath the yard was positioned a network of rooms, pits and tunnels, some of them filled with machinery. Above it were workshops.*

The 'porch' referred to here seems most likely to be the main gatehouse to the Abbey property at the end of Abbey Strand rather than the porch of the church itself. The position of the gatehouse (described in the introduction to Holyrood), facing the Abbey but a good distance from it, fits closely with the description of the stage in the yard, the views from the royal stand and an arena with room enough for two thousand spectators.

*The procession down from the Castle was a triumphant one ... despite a shower of rain; and the comfort of the royal stand, when they reached it, drew exclamations from the eminent visitors. They gazed at the face of the Abbey before them, hung with arras and garlands. They studied the silks of the awnings, the veiled and silent box of the stage in the centre below them ... From the well of the Abbey arena there arose the buzz of a beehive: the expectant murmur of two thousand curious souls ... the curtains raced back from the four walls of the stage ... Behind them was Paradise ... It had begun.*

# Excursions

## Craigmillar Castle

*Crowning its own hill to the south-east of Edinburgh ... Craigmillar was halfway between Roslin and Leith ... you could see the Pentland hills and the sea ... [and also] the crag of Arthur's Seat and the David's Tower of Edinburgh Castle, upon which Craigmillar was modelled.* (Gem, Pt 2, Ch 17)

Uninhabited and partly ruined, Craigmillar is a stunning medieval castle, which lies in parkland on the south side of Edinburgh and once lay outside the city. The Preston family built the tower house in the 14th century at a similar time to David's Tower, with common principles of construction and defence. With five floors from the dungeon to a rooftop that affords spectacular views of Edinburgh, Craigmillar is a perfect castle to

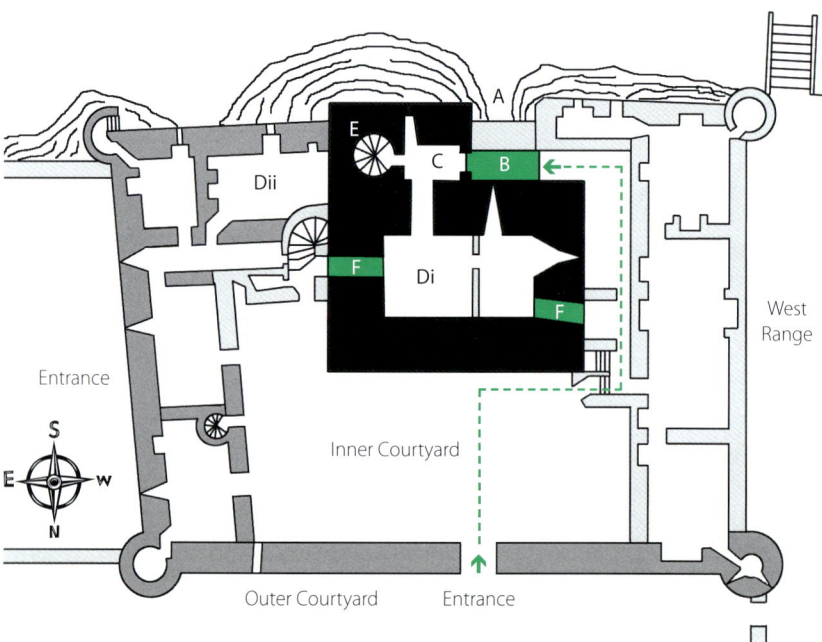

- Tower, built before *Gemini*
- Possibly built before *Gemini*
- Built later than *Gemini*
- -- Nicholas's route into the castle

**I CRAIGMILLAR CASTLE**
A    Chasm
B    Site of Drawbridge
C    Main entrance in 15th century
Di    Storeroom (temporary hall)
Dii    Alternate temporary hall
E    Main Stair
F    Passages cut late 15th/early 16th century

explore: full of twists and turns, and of unexpected treasures.

It was built with defence in mind. The main entrance was a double doorway on the south side, at the cliff edge and across a natural chasm. It was approached via a wooden drawbridge. Subsequent infilling has left bedrock still showing through in places. Extra wings and layers of defence were added to match the status and needs of the owners. A curtain wall, built in the 15th century on the three sides not protected by the cliff, enclosed a courtyard. An outer wall was added in the 16th century to encompass more land and a chapel. The East and West Ranges, probably overlying earlier structures, date to the 16th and 17th centuries respectively.

Craigmillar Castle is the setting in *Gemini* for David Simpson's attempt to poison the king and implicate Adorne. John of Mar is badly affected by the poison and runs amok. Readers might like to visualise those events.

### The Affair of the Poisoned Soup – *Gemini* (Pt 2, Ch 17 and 18)

From the Visitor Centre you pass through the 16th-century wall and alongside the 15th-century curtain wall to the doorway into the inner courtyard that Nicholas and his party would have encountered.

*The Prestons' heraldic device, repeated all over the castle, was argent three unicorn heads erased sable ...*

The device can still be seen over the doorway to the courtyard and in many other places throughout the castle.

The main entrance to the Tower House is on the far side of the building and is accessed from the right far corner of the Inner Courtyard (see map). When Tobie arrives for what he knows is going to be a difficult evening:

*[He] climbed up to the drawbridge and stepped over with the kind of emotion he imagined Nicholas and Willie must have felt long ago, when the curtains swirled back to introduce their famous play.*

The spiral staircase inside this entrance was the main stair of the castle. The king is upstairs, feasting in the Hall and they are shown to another room to wait, close enough to hear the music:

*There were two public apartments in use, of which the upper was that presided over by the King, with his host and his house-guests and family. Below was the temporary hall filled by local guests like themselves.*

Tobie notices 'bevies of Prestons' as well as numerous others so the room was a reasonable size. It is difficult to be completely certain which room Dorothy Dunnett intended but we can speculate. Once inside, turn through a door on your left that leads to a complicated room signposted as a storeroom. A dividing wall in the middle is a later addition and the barrel vaulted ceiling belonged to a room above. Nicholas may have waited here. Alternatively, if Dorothy Dunnett assumed that the doorways in the east and west walls already existed (they were cut some time in the late 15th or early 16th century), she might have had in mind one of the two chambers through the door that leads to the East Range.

When Nicholas and his party are called to attend the king in the hall, Gelis finds her long skirts an encumbrance on the stairs.

*Jodi was leading the way to the stairs, which were of the steeply spiral variety that led Gelis to fear for the seams of her skirts. She clutched them, twisting, and climbed.*

At the next level a door to your left leads to the Great Hall. To that door's left the original entrance to the old kitchen has left its mark on the stone.

The Great Hall is one of the most intact rooms in the whole castle. It was originally the lower of two chambers, having a painted wooden ceiling resting on the corbels about half way up the wall. The walls were decorated with painted plaster. When Nicholas and his party enter the hall, a screen had been erected to allow servants to traverse that end of the hall to and from the kitchen without being seen.

*... heat and noise pulsed from beyond the carved screen that guarded the end of the Great Hall of Craigmillar. The hall, being only thirty-five feet in length, became easily crowded, despite its deep window embrasures; and its low painted ceiling repeated all that it heard.*

The window embrasures are still evident, as is the large fireplace. The high table would have been placed at that end of the room, the most important seat being in the centre. As Nicholas, Gelis, *et al* arrive:

*Perceiving the newcomers, the King ... walked to his chair of state in front of the chimney-piece ... His guests presented themselves at the foot of the dais.*

Despite the relatively luxurious surroundings Dorothy Dunnett describes the smells that dominated the room with the 'reek in the hall' made worse by:

*bowls of black, pungent soup which the King drank earnestly dry, sending Sandy for more. The kitchen was just outside the screen.*

The room off the Great Hall (to the left as you came in) was the kitchen and although evidence of the ovens remains it was later altered into a bedchamber. It is now signposted as Queen Mary's Room but, although she visited twice in 1560s, it is unlikely ever to have been so.

Most of the ill-effects, physical and political, of David Simpson's plot are forestalled by Nicholas and Anselm Adorne but John of Mar is seriously affected by the poison:

*[Adorne said] 'His sight is blurred and his senses distorted: he does not know what is real. It is dangerous. He should be watched until he recovers.'*

Mar breaks from the men trying to restrain him and, his judgement impaired, runs from the room and up through the castle.

*... John of Mar burst through the door to the turnpike. There, instead of descending, he set off, screaming and lurching, to scale the spiral steps to the roof. The flat, stone-flagged roof from which you could see the sea, and Edinburgh Castle.*

Men rush after him to find and keep him safe. To follow the route, go back to the turnpike stairs and climb up through two more storeys until the door opens out to the battlements at the top of the castle. To your left lies the stone flagged roof; ahead is the spectacular view. From here it is easy to appreciate that the fear of John of Mar coming to harm is very real.

At the same time, Nicholas frees himself and Tobie.

*[and a] hand, belonging to Nicholas, gripped Tobie hard and propelled him likewise to the door. As men bounded up the stairs, he and Nicholas bounded down. At the foot they saw no sign of David, but Henry de St Pol sprinting up with three horses.*

Later in the book, when he 'fell into a frenzy', John of Mar is kept in Craigmillar Castle. Nicholas and Tobie visit him, and manage to calm him somewhat. Soon after, he is moved to Tobie's house in the Canongate.

## Leith

*Close at hand was the mouth of the river Leith, timber-shored on each side, with some coasting vessels and a quantity of fishing-boats within a breakwater made of rough stobs and boulders. To left and right of the river stood a smoky collection of thatched cabins, kailyards, wood and stone warehouses, and a number of tallish houses of a more ambitious sort, with kilns and bakehouses and wooden sheds round about them ... For this was the haven of Edinburgh. This was the greatest port in the kingdom.* (UH, Pt 1, Ch 2)

Leith lies on the shore of the coastal River Forth and is Edinburgh's port. Once separate from Edinburgh with numerous small settlements in between, it remained an independent burgh until 1920. There is evidence of settlement there from the 12th century and Edinburgh and Canongate were both granted trading rights. The Water of Leith, a river that rises in the Pentland Hills, runs through Edinburgh and flows into the Forth at

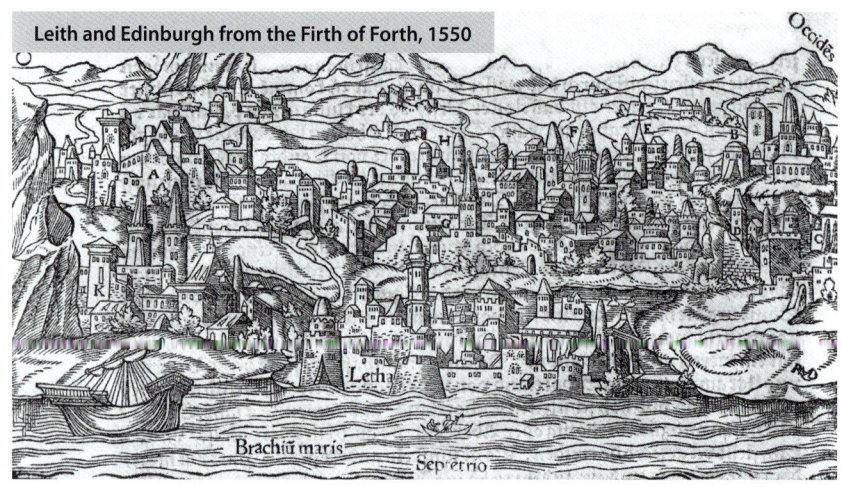

Leith and Edinburgh from the Firth of Forth, 1550

Leith. The river separates the town into North and South Leith. There have been many phases of renewal and rebuilding and the port now extends far beyond the earlier shoreline. There is very little to remind the visitor of the Renaissance period except the views and vistas from the shore.

### Nicholas and Leith

> They were all freshly dressed … Nicholas and [Julius] from the clothes they kept over the river, where Nicholas had leased some convenient rooms in North Leith. (UH, Pt 1, Ch 3)

From the moment Nicholas arrives in Leith he forges a strong association with the town. He rents from Archie Berecrofts in North Leith, which was the smaller, richer part of the town owned by the Abbots of Holyrood and reached by a ford. The first bridge was built there in 1496. At that time, ships unloaded at The Shore, which was the harbourside.

He has warehouses there, conducts much of his trade in the town and spends increasing amounts of time there, attending to his business. With Gelis and Jodi, Nicholas returns to Scotland in *To Lie With Lions* in style:

> The grand entrance took place at Leith, as Nicholas wanted. His caravel rowed into harbour, its sails shipped, its sides washed and shining, its banners taut, its trumpets piping and blaring … men stood arrayed on the riverside wharf: the magnates of Scotland, come to welcome their Knight of the Unicorn. (TLWL, Pt 1, Ch 9)

In *Gemini*, Nicholas's entrance is more circumspect and he and Andro Wodman leave the ship to go secretly to Edinburgh. Leith and Edinburgh were connected by two main roads, which ran through the small villages in between. The Wester Road ran initially upstream along the Water of Leith towards Leith Wynd and continued roughly on the line of the modern Bonnington and Broughton Roads. The Easter Road (which still exists in part) ran more directly to Holyrood.

> *They had chosen the western, riverside route to the town, because it kept to the Holyrood bailery, and touched the busy hamlet of Bonnington, which led to the Canongate, and was tenanted by yet other Crawfords. Also, being longer, the way was less apt to be plagued like the Easter Road, with wealthy pack-trains, or ox-wagons stuck in the mud ...* (Gem, Pt 1, Ch 1)

They were ambushed en route, supposedly by de Salmeton and his men, the attack disguised as a feud between local oystermen.

---

**THE WATER OF LEITH WALKWAY**
This is a foot and cycle path which runs for 12 miles alongside the river and through Edinburgh. Walkers can join on various points along its route, and in Leith access is signposted at the Shore. From there it runs through areas named after villages that used to be outside the city: Bonnington, Cannonmills, Stockbridge, Dean Village, Roseburn and Colinton. The Walkway takes in many points of interest, and its green spaces are a home for wildlife. There is a visitor centre in Slateford run by the Conservation Trust that maintains the river and Walkway.

---

### King's Wark

> *The King's Wark ... A royal enclave, in which the King's ordnance could be stored, and where the Court could stay when travelling.* (UH, Pt 1, Ch 2)

Built *c.* 1433, this royal building was at once a garrison, armoury and residence. It lay next to the Water of Leith on the corner of what is now The Shore and Bernard Street, and although the current tenements are 18th century in origin, the restaurant on the site is named after the royal residence.

### Lamb's House

> *Lamb had the biggest house. He was a merchant, and used to putting up travellers, in the same way that Jehan Metteneye's own home in Bruges acted as hostelry for incoming traders; as Adorne's own palatial mansion did for others more princely.* (UH, Pt 1, Ch 2)

For centuries the Lamb family were important merchants in Leith. Lamb's House is one of the oldest in the area, but the current building in Water Street, just back from the Water of Leith to the east, dates to the 17th century. Although not generally open to the public, there are occasional Open Doors days.
    Kathi and Adorne have arranged to stay at John Lamb's house when they arrive in Leith in *The Unicorn Hunt*. However, finding the owner not at home, they are redirected to the beach where James III, his siblings and his court are at sport.

### Leith Links

> ... Metteneye and Adorne went with the children ... picking their way east through the cabins, the poultry and fish-creels to the rough grazing that ran down to the sea, where ... half a dozen middle-aged burghers ... swished through the grass with thick sticks, as if beating for hares. (UH, Pt 1, Ch 2)

They become involved with golfers playing 'kolf', an early name for the game played with sticks, hitting a ball at a target. The open land used to run clear down to the dunes and thence the sea but it is now an inland public park.

Kathi finds her host and the young royals at play on the then adjoining Leith Strand, a long beach that has disappeared with the changes to the coastline since the 15th century. However the vista from Portobello beach, approximately 3 miles east along the coast, gives a good impression of the scene she describes.

> [Kathi] saw the beach, dry near at hand, and further away firm and shining and pocked like a ploughed field with hoof-marks. Beyond was the grey sea, and far beyond that, the pale shores and blue hills of the land on the other side of the estuary. Near at hand from the right came the sound of low drumming ... The beach was far longer than she had imagined. It ran glistening and yellow-grey into the distance, where a cloud of silvery spume announced the approach of a massed group of riders, vying with one another in and out of the surf. (UH, Pt 1, Ch 2)

### Lymond and Leith

It is most likely that Lymond arrives in Leith first before entering Edinburgh by stealth at the beginning of *The Game of Kings*. Later, Richard plans to take him there to escape to the Continent rather than face trial.

> 'You're not going for trial. You'll travel to Leith, and from there get out of the country.' (GoK, Pt 3, Ch 1)

### Musselburgh (The Battle of Pinkie)

The Site of the Battle of Pinkie

> On Saturday, September 10th, the English Protector Somerset and his army met the combined Scottish forces on the field of Pinkie, outside Edinburgh, and smashed them to pieces in a defeat as dire as any the Scots had suffered since Flodden. (GoK, Pt 1, Ch 1)

66

The last battle of the Rough Wooing, and the last major battle in the wars between England and Scotland, the Battle of Pinkie was a disastrous defeat for the Scots.

Leith had suffered damage at the hands of the English army in 1544 but worse was to come in September 1547:

> ... *after Pinkie, when the army broke; and the [the English and their allies] flew along the Leith sands, and the Holyrood road, and the Dalkeith road, hawking men with their swords like butterflies.* (GoK, Pt 1, Ch 7)

The site of the conflict is just south of the town of Musselburgh (5 miles to the east of Leith along the A1), but the camps of the two armies encompassed part of modern Edinburgh. There is a battlefield walk, with interpretive boards, which leads over the area and begins at the Roman Bridge in Musselburgh.

## Roslin/Rosslyn

> *Nicholas had been to Roslin Castle before, deep in its wooded glen in the loop of a river, ten miles south of Edinburgh.* (Gem, Pt 1, Ch 4)

Whilst the modern spelling of the names of the village (Roslin), chapel (Rosslyn) and castle (Rosslyn or Roslin) are different, they come from the same root, describing a rocky promontory and a waterfall. Dorothy Dunnett uses Roslin throughout. Both chapel and castle are built on land still owned by the St Clair family.

> *Former Vikings, former Normans, the Sinclairs all ran to fairness and bulk ...* (Gem, Pt 1, Ch 4)

The name St Clair is used interchangeably with Sinclair in Renaissance sources. Dorothy Dunnett uses the name Sinclair for Nicholas's contemporaries and St Clair only for their forebears, although the family today uses French version.

> *The first Sinclair to cross to England from St Clair-sur-Epte had fought at the Battle of Hastings under William the Conqueror, who was his cousin, and descended from the same Orkney Jarl.* (Gem, Pt 5, Ch 47)

Nicholas meets several important members of the Sinclair family, who can trace their Norse lineage back, in Dorothy Dunnett terms, to *King Hereafter*:

> '... *They say you can hear the voice of Thorfinn in the wind ... His son Paul had a granddaughter who carried the Earldom of Orkney to the Scots Earl of Atholl ... a few generations on brought it to the Earl of Strathearn ... And a girl ... gave the Earldom with her hand to a Sinclair ...*' (TLWL, Pt 3, Ch 21)

By Nicholas's time, they were a powerful family who had extensive lands throughout Scotland, money and political influence.

## Roslin Village

The village of Roslin lies 10 miles south of Edinburgh, and is accessible by bus or car from the city. Its origins lie in the homes of the masons brought into the area to build Rosslyn Chapel. Nicholas stayed the night there before visiting the castle.

> Nicholas remembered the cabins, put up when the new church of St Matthew was started, and since grown into a small village for the wrights, the masons, the plasterers who were slowly perfecting it, at a speed dictated by the input of interest, money and indeed whimsy by the reigning Sinclairs of Roslin. (Gem, Pt 1, Ch 4)

## Rosslyn Chapel

The chapel can be found clearly signposted to the south of the village.

Sir William St Clair, Earl of Orkney, father of Sir Oliver and Betha Sinclair and uncle of Phemie Dunbar founded the chapel in 1446. The church that stands today represents only the choir of the miniature cathedral that was envisioned by its founder. Dedicated to St Matthew, this was a Collegiate Chapel and Nicholas visits when it is still under construction.

> The nave, not yet started, was meant to be ninety feet long, positing a church as big as St Giles. They had been building for thirty years and had got the choir nearly done, all forty feet of it. (Gem, Pt 1, Ch 4)

Although the original design was never completed, the chapel is a masterpiece of stonework. The exterior sports flying buttresses bearing the founder's name and the date of its building. Inside, it appears that every surface and pillar is decorated with carvings.

> This ode to the Sinclairs, truncated at either end, aspirationally based on the plan of Solomon's Temple, was not quite of the dimensions to carry the emblems with which it was loaded, coated and smothered, as in a kiosk in Tabriz. Except that here, you would say, the carvers had not been of uniform mind, or indeed of uniform training. The clustered shafts, the carved arcades, the canopied niches, the traceried windows, the figured and foliaceous capitals, the storeyed entablatures celebrated, as was to be expected, the triumphs of every known member of the family St Clair ... (Gem, Pt 1, Ch 4)

Rosslyn Chapel

The carvings are indeed disparate in form and subject, some biblical and others more secular in origin. The Seven Virtuous Acts and Seven Sins can be

Carving of Bagpipes, Rosslyn Chapel

found in the ceiling of the south aisle. There are 110 green man carvings in the chapel, and although a pagan symbol, they are not uncommon in churches of the period. Eight dragons coil at the base of the apprentice pillar near the end of the south aisle, a possible link to the eight dragons of Neifelheim, and a reminder of the family's Norse roots.

> *But among the armorial devices, the country-style Biblical figures – the Dance of Death; the Seven Virtuous Acts – were other strange faces, wild and pagan and snarling, which had more to do with the dark empire of the great Viking Rognvald the Mighty, Jarl of the Orkneys, from whom all Sinclairs claimed descent.* (Gem, Pt 1, Ch 4)

A set of stairs at the east end of the south aisle leads down to the Sacristy. This was probably part of an earlier church that stood on the same site, but in Nicholas's day was used by the masons as a workshop. Nicholas spends an evening there with mason Tam Cochrane, his crew and Will Roger on the way to Rosslyn Castle.

> *'Down' meant down the steps to the sacristy, the drawing-office, the booming underground cavern with the stools and the trestles and the mattresses where the arguing, the gossip, the eating and drinking went on as the work progressed and different experts came to serve their time in the dusty gloom far above. One day it would be the awful, chill heart of the church. Now it was the place for refreshment, creation and recreation: a haven of light and warmth under the ground. Trust masons.* (Gem, Pt 1, Ch 4)

Working diagrams still cover the walls, and the ceiling is decorated with the engrailed cross of the St Clair family.

The Lady Chapel at the east end of the church, where the four original altars stood, is heavily decorated, and bears carvings of angels playing a variety of instruments, including the bagpipes.

> ... In [Will Roger's] arms were a rebec, a recorder and a set of bagpipes ... Cochrane said, grinning, 'See our model. We want some angels with instruments up on one of those capitals. About there ...' (Gem, Pt 1, Ch 4)

The chapel has attracted a great deal of mythology, from the resting place of the Holy Grail to Templar gold. What is known, however, is that it was for many years the final resting place for the St Clair family. In *Gemini* the service for Phemie Dunbar takes place there after her death in childbirth.

> And inside they knelt, still in silence, before the casket that stood at the altar, and looked upon the calm, closed face of the child's mother, Euphemia Dunbar, lady of March, lying in death. (Gem, Pt 1, Ch 11)

## Rosslyn Castle

Nicholas visits Rosslyn Castle several times because it is the home of Sir Oliver ('Nowie') Sinclair. It is still a peaceful and beautiful setting:

> By day, the easiest way to the castle was the low one, through the deep gorge and over the bridge by the waterfall that gave Roslin its name. In wintry darkness, a band of lightly inebriated masons chose the high path which skirted the valley and, passing hamlet and chapel, plunged down to the keep from above. The path did not go all the way: just before the castle doors, a chasm had been cut in the rock, offering monitored access by means of a high, vaulted bridge with a fifty-foot drop. There was also a turreted gatehouse with guards in it. (Gem, Pt 1, Ch 4)

Phemie Dunbar lives here during her pregnancy.

> The place Betha took him to was warm and bright, a little apartment of several rooms, the first of which had thick paned glass in the windows and a table and priedieu, and a leather chair and a stool set before a real fireplace. (Gem, Pt 1, Ch 4)

The castle, now mostly a ruin, can be accessed from the south of the chapel car park. This is the 'high path' approached via a 16th-century stone bridge over the gorge cut by the Sinclairs. The bridge replaced a wooden drawbridge that gave entrance to the castle at one of its upper floors. The castle stands in a loop of the River North Esk and was five storeys high. The entrance and western curtain wall were present in Nicholas's day; however, the castle was almost destroyed during Hertford's invasion in 1544. Restoration and rebuilding took place in the east range in the 17th century. What remains of the castle is private and can be rented as self-catering accommodation.

It is also possible to go down the very steep path (the 'low path') into Roslin Glen, now a country park, and view the castle from beside the River North Esk. From there the restored east wing can be seen to sit on an enormous wall that rises from the glen floor.

# Places of Interest

## The National Museum of Scotland

This museum is on Chambers Street and a visit could easily be combined with visits to the Grassmarket, the Lawnmarket or the upper part of the High Street.

This plan indicates the most important artefacts of interest to Dunnett readers. They are currently housed (2015) in the Kingdom of the Scots Gallery on the ground floor (Level 1). This is most easily accessed from the Tower Entrance, and the key to the map follows a suggested route round the gallery.

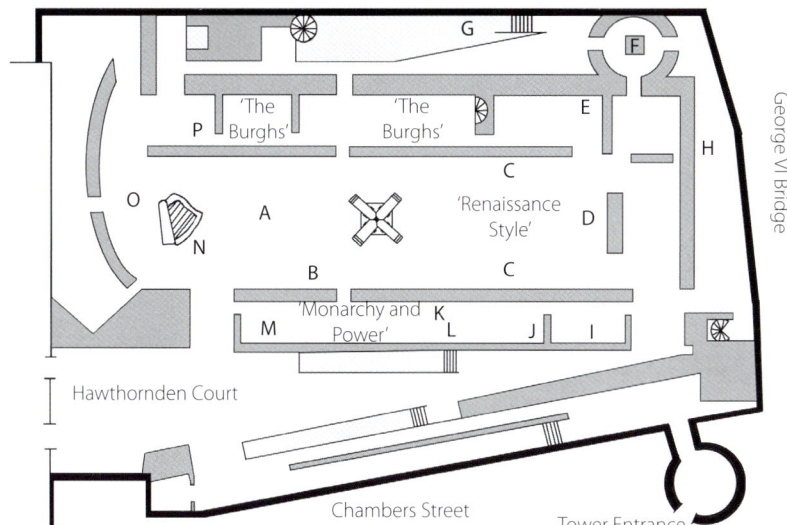

### J THE NATIONAL MUSEUM OF SCOTLAND

A   Weaponry and Coins
B   Lochleven Wall Hanging
C   16th-century furniture, doors and wall panelling
D   Mary, Queen of Scots: artefacts and replica of sarcophagus
E   Mary de Guise: wall panels and decorative stonework from her palace:

*In Mary de Guise's palace the tapers took fire from room to room, and the Queen Dowager moved with her maids to the audience chamber* (GoK, Pt 4, Ch 4)

F   Holyrood and the Church of the Trinity: plate, carving and lectern
G   Fetternear Banner and the Cult of the Holy Blood:

*So Bruges found itself occupied by the Court, and witnessing the three-day gathering of the eleventh Chapter of the Duke's Golden Fleece Order, and the Holy Blood procession on top, with every street filled with banners and choirs and platforms with actors and singers.* (SoG, Ch 41)

71

**Places of Interest**

H St Giles' and the Church of the Trinity: prayer books, a stool and communion cups
I Crime and punishment
J The Douglas Banner and 16th-century light armour often favoured by Lymond:

*[Lymond said]... My personal cargo is a twenty-five-pound helmet, a brigantine jacket and a sword ... (DK, Pt 2, Ch 3)*

K Stewart/Stuart monarchs
L Border control: Scotland and England, artefacts from Threave Castle
M 16th-century weapons
N Mary, Queen of Scots: Clarsach (harp)
O Norse artefacts including the Lewis Chessmen:

*They were chessmen, so old that the whalebone had yellowed and there were cracks in the knights' shields and the queens' tunics and pigtails. There were runes cut very small in the base. (TLWL, Pt 4, Ch 40)*

P Mungo Tennant's Lintel from Gosford Close:

*[Mungo] led the way to the apartment beneath the stairs where lived Mungo's great sow, the badge of his house, the pet and idiotic pig's apple of his eye (GoK, Opening Gambit).*

### The National Gallery of Scotland

Highlights for the Dunnett reader are housed in the Early Italian and European Gallery (Upper Level North). Enter by the main entrance and climb the stairs directly ahead.

Hugo van der Goes's Trinity Altarpiece was commissioned by Provost Edward Bonkle (natural father of John), who appears on the right when the panels are closed.

*Before them leaned part of the altar-piece for the Trinity Church, painted in a haze of alcohol by Hugo vander Goes ... Before a dazzling organ ... knelt Edward Bonkle, provost of the Collegiate Church of the Holy Trinity, Edinburgh. The Provost's body was solid. His surplice and amice fell into exquisite lines. His face was, to the life, that of the good-natured father and businessman Canon Bonkle, to whom the King's Flemish mother had entrusted her church. (*Gem*, Pt 3, Ch 25)*

Dorothy Dunnett refers to the completed picture, on loan from the Trinity Church to St Michael's at Linlithgow for Adorne's funeral.

*The anonymous painted prince at this altar, piously kneeling, was not nine-year-old James ... Nor would anyone ever admit, now, that it might be Albany, possible heir to the throne. (*Gem*, Pt 5, Ch 53)*

Gerlach Flicke's Lord Grey of Wilton is dated to 1547, when *The Game of Kings* begins, and is thought to be William Grey, 13th Baron of Wilton

*Sitting at his temporary desk, sleek, pink and picturesque, hair and beard a silver perfection above splendid riding clothes, he was in as petulant a mood as a gentleman of quality can be. (*GoK*, Pt 1, Ch 2)*

Further 15th- and 16th-century works can be found in rooms 1 and 2.

## The Scottish National Portrait Gallery

The Gallery building in the New Town is a Victorian masterpiece and its facade is adorned with sculptures of significant Scottish historical figures. The entranceway frieze depicts the monarchs of Scotland as a procession in order of date with the 15th- and 16th-century monarchs immediately ahead. James III and Queen Margaret are painted in the outfits from the Trinity Altarpiece. On the balcony a number of paintings mark significant moments in Scottish history.

The Reformation Gallery contains the 16th-century paintings and there are iconic images on permanent display. A portrait of Mary de Guise shows her as a young woman, some years before Tom Erskine's observations.

> *Regal, humourless, briskly prosaic, the Queen Dowager of Scotland ... was a big woman, boxed in quilting in spite of the weather ... The Queen Mother was a subtle woman, and not Scots. The thick oils of statesmanship ran in Mary of Guise's veins, and she rarely handed through the door what she could throw in by the cat's hole.* (QP, *Pt 1, Ch 1*)

There are two posthumous portraits of Mary, Queen of Scots and portraits of her three husbands.

## The National Library of Scotland

Dorothy Dunnett used the National Library of Scotland extensively for her research. For fifteen years she was also a Trustee. This is the largest library in Scotland, and contains texts, maps and visual archives.

In addition, the Dorothy Dunnett Archive contains a large number of her papers including gems relevant to her writing. Details on how to access this can be found on the Dorothy Dunnett Society website. Anyone can apply for a reader's card, and it is also possible to access some of the library's holdings online.

# Further Reading

For readers wishing to find out more about the history of Edinburgh the following texts are recommended:

Coghill, Hamish, *Lost Edinburgh*. Birlinn Ltd, 2008.
Fry, Michael, *A History of Edinburgh*. Pan Books, 2011.
Marshall, Rosalind K, *St Giles' – The Dramatic Story of a Great Church and its People*. St Andrews Press, 2009.
Grant, James, *Cassell's Old and New Edinburgh*. Cassel, Petter, Galpin & Co, 1880.

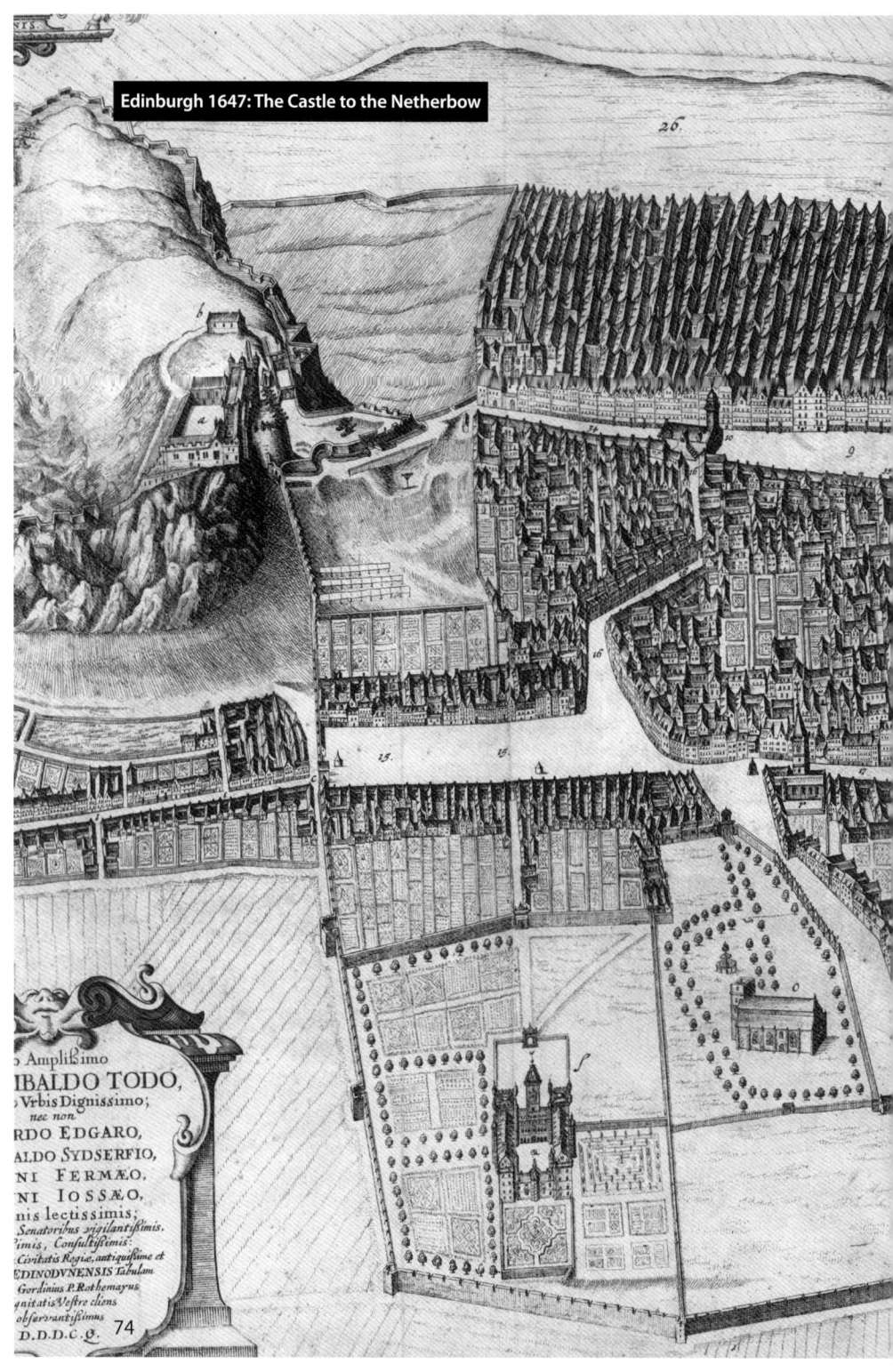

Edinburgh 1647: The Castle to the Netherbow

# Edinburgh 1647: The Netherbow to Holyrood

Loca Urbis notatu digna.
a. Arx.
b. Arcis capella.
c. Porta occidentalis.
d. Porta societatis.
e. Porta figulina.
f. Porta bovina.
g. Porta plateæ Sanctæ Mariæ.
h. Inferioris arcus porta.
i. Lethensis plateæ porta.
k. Porta aquatica.
l. Templum prope arcem.
m. Templum magnum, seu S. Ægidy.
n. Templum ad Libram.
o. Templum occidentale, seu franciscanorum cum cœmiterio publico.
p. Templum collegiatum.
q. Templum dominæ de Yester.
r. S. Magdalenæ capella.
s. Ptochii Zenodochion, cum hortis.
t. Trinitatis gerontochium.
u. S. Pauli ædificium.
w. Academia.
x. Schola latina.
y. Rudera templi S. Mariæ in campis.
z. Templum abbatiæ S. crucis cum cœmiterio.
1. Suburbium portæ occidentalis.
2. Suburbium societatis.
3. Suburbium plateæ figulinæ.
4. Suburbium plateæ S. Mariæ.
5. Suburbium de Plaisanc.
6. Niniani suburbium seu mendicorum platea.
7. Suburbium Bristounum.
8. Suburbium plateæ Canonicæ.
9. Platea suprema ab arce ad palatium.
10. Domus Libræ.
11. Carcer publicus.
12. Crux supremæ plateæ.
13. Libra.
14. Arcus inferior.
15. Platea fori equini.
16. Platea arctioris arcus.
17. Platea bovina.
18. Ædificia societatis simul cum hortis.
19. Forum farinarium.
20. Comitiorum regni domus.
21. Domus senatoria urbis.
22. Forum piscatorium.
23. Macellum.
24. Ergastlorium.
25. Urbis mœnia.
26. Lacus borealis.
27. Rupes boreales, seu Nigelli rupes.
28. Macellum plateæ Canonicæ.
30. Crux plateæ Canonicæ.
31. Sphæristerium plateæ Canonicæ.
32. Prætorium plateæ Canonicæ.
33. Palatium regium S. crucis, cum hortis.

Nomina vicorum in latere urbis Australi, qui incolarum multitudine et ædificiorum splendore plateas æquant.

34. Vicus
35. Vicus
36. Vicus
38. Vicus
39. Vicus
40. Vicus
41. Vicus
42. Vicus
43. Vicus
44. Vicus
45. Vicus
46. Vicus
47. Vicus
48. Vicus
49. Vicus
50. Vicus
51. Vicus
52. Vicus
53. Vicus
54. Vicus
55. Vicus
56. Vicus

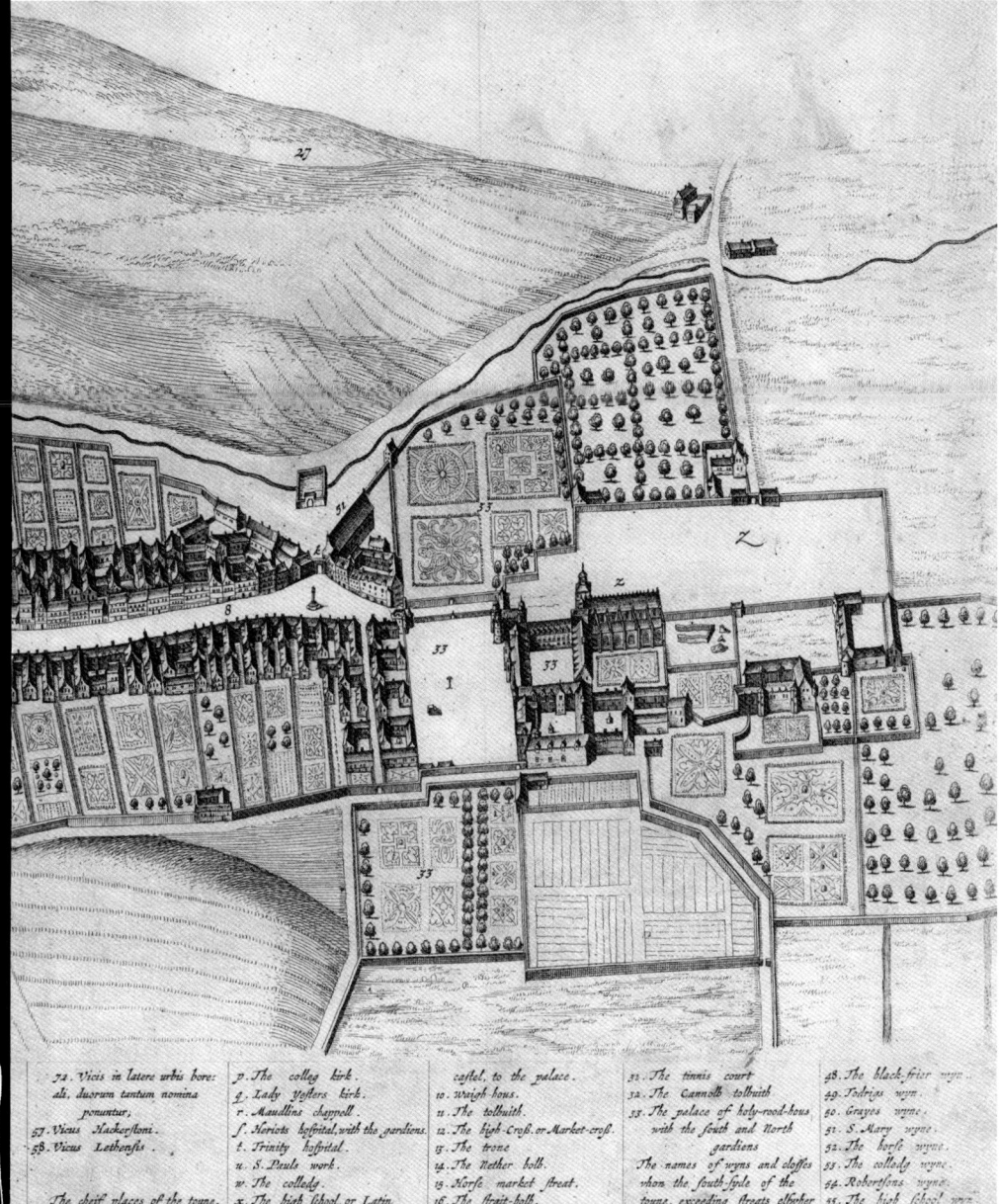

| | | castel, to the palace. | 31. The tinnis court | 48. The black-frier wyn |
|---|---|---|---|---|
| 72. Vicis in latere urbis bore- | p. The colleg kirk | 10. Waigh hous. | 32. The Cannoll tolbuith | 49. Todrigs wyn. |
| alis, duorum tantum nomina | q. Lady Yesters kirk | 11. The tolbuith | 33. The palace of holy-rood-hous | 50. Grayes wyn. |
| ponuntur. | r. Maudlins chappell | 12. The high-Cross, or Market-cross. | with the south and North | 51. S. Mary wyne. |
| 57. Vicus Hackerstoni. | s. Heriots hospital, with the gardiens. | 13. The trone | gardiens | 52. The horse wyne. |
| 58. Vicus Lethensis. | t. Trinity hospital. | 14. The Nether bolh. | The names of wyns and closses | 53. The colledg wyne. |
| | u. S. Pauls work. | 15. Horse market street. | whan the south-syde of the | 54. Robertsons wyne. |
| The cheif places of the toune. | w. The colledg | 16. The strait-bolh. | toune, exceeding streats elswher | 55. The high school wyn |
| a. The castel. | x. The high school, or Latin | 17. The kow-gait. | in the number of indwellers | 56. Beths wyne. |
| b. The castel chappel. | schoole. | 18. The society with the gardiens. | and fairnes of houses. | Of the 76. wyns and |
| c. The west port. | y. S. Mary of the fields | 19. Meil market. | 34. Carrers closs | whon the North Syde |
| d. The society port. | or the kirk of field. | 20. The parlament hous. | 35. Libbertons wyne | toune. ther ar onl |
| e. The potter-raw port. | z. The Abbey kirk, with the | 21. The toun Counsel hous. | 36. Fosters wyn. | two, to wit, |
| f. The kow-gait port. | kirkyaird. | 22. The fish Markett. | 38. S. Monans wyne. | 57. Hackerstons wyn. |
| g. S. Mary wyn port. | 1. West port suburbs. | 23. The flesh Markett. | 39. Fish market wyne. | 58. Lieth wyn. |
| h. The nether bolh port. | 2. Society suburbs. | 24. The Correction hous. | 40. Borthwiks wyne. | |
| i. Lieth wyn port. | 3. Potter raw suburbs. | 25. The toune wall. | 41. Cons closs. | |
| k. The watter port. | 4. St. Mary wyn suburbs. | 26. The North loch. | 42. Bels wyn. | |
| l. The kirk in the castel hill. | 5. Suburbs of Plaisanc | 27. The North craigs, or | 43. Stoven Laws closs | |
| m. The great kirk, or S. Gilles | 6. S. Ringens suburbs, or the | Neils craigs. | 44. Pobls wyn | |
| n. The tron kerk kerk. | begger-raw. | 28. The flesh stocks in the | 45. Morlins wyne. | |
| o. The west kirk or gray-frier | 7. Bristolh suburbs. | Canno-gait. | 46. Needris wyn. | |
| kirk, with the burial plac. | 8. Suburbs of the Cannoll-gait. | 30. The Canno cross. | 47. Dicksons closs. | |
| | 9. The high street, from the | | | |

## Glossary

| | |
|---|---|
| Bow or Port | Gate or entrance |
| Close | Generic term for any narrow street or walkway descending the slope to north or south of the ridge that forms the Royal Mile. The following terms are now used interchangeably: |
| | Close: narrow entrance to private property, sometimes secured or gated which led between the buildings, called lands (qv) |
| | Court: Wider space (courtyard) leading to private property |
| | Entry: entrance to private property |
| | Vennel: narrow public lane leading to open ground |
| | Wynd: public lane wide enough for a cart |
| Court | See: Close |
| Craimes (or Kraimes) | Stalls set up on the north wall of St Giles'. |
| Entry | See: Close |
| Gait or Gate | Walk or thoroughfare |
| Kirk | Church |
| Kirkyard | Churchyard |
| Land | House or building or the piece of ground the building is on |
| Loch | A lake |
| Luckenbooth | A luckenbooth is a locked booth or shop. The Luckenbooths (with an upper case 'L') were a specific row of shops next to St Giles'. |
| Mercat Cross | Cross marking where the main market took place |
| Tenement | Building in multiple occupation |
| Toft | Plot of land stretching down the slope with a house on the narrow frontage on the street |
| Tolbooth | Place to pay tolls, court house, jail and meeting place |
| Tron | Weighing machine used to regulate trade and for taxation purposes |
| Trance | Passage between closes off the main street |
| Vennel | See: Close |
| Wynd | See: Close |

# Index

Entries in **bold** are headings within the text

## A

**Abbey** (Holyrood)  6, 7, 12, 19, 50, 53, 55–57, **58**, 59
Abbey Strand  2, 56, 57, 59
Abbot Henry  29
Adam Acheson  24
**Advocate's Close  43**, 44
**Affair of the Poisoned Soup, The**  3, **61**–63
Agnes, Lady Herries  58
Albany (Alexander 'Sandy' Stewart, Duke of Albany)  19, 61, 72
Andro Wodman  54, 64
Anselm Adorne  30, 31, 61, 63, 65, 66, 72
Anselm Sersanders  51, 54
Archie (of) Berecrofts  51, 53, 54, 64
Arthur's Seat  3, 59, 60

## B

Banco di Niccolò. *See* Ca' Niccolò
Bank Street  2, 24, 25, 43
**Battle of Pinkie**  3, **66**, 67
**Bell's Wynd**  31, **42**, 43
**Berecrofts House, The**  52, **53**
Betha Sinclair  68, 70
Blackfriars Monastery  9, 46, 47, 51
**Blackfriars Street and Wynd  46**, 47
Bonnington  4, 64, 65
Booth Raw. *See* Luckenbooths
Bristo Port  9, 24
Broughton  4, 7, 45, 64
**Bruce's Close**  11, 43–45
Buccleuch  3, 18, 21, 23, 27, 31, 39, 40–43, 50
**Buccleuch's death**  23, 27, 39, **40**–42
**Buccleuch's house**  40–**43**
Buith Raw. *See* Luckenbooths
**Butter Tron**  25, **27**, 28, 44

## C

Calton Hill  3, 44, 46, 53
**Ca' Niccolò**  49, **51**, 52
**Canongate**  2–4, 6–9, 12, 13, 44, 49, **50**–56, 59, 63, 65
**Canongate Kirk**  52, **55**
**Canongate Tolbooth**  52, **54**
Canonmills  4, 45
**Castlehill** (Castle Hill)  2, 12, **24**–27, 43
Castle Rock  3, 5, 7, 9, 10, 14, 18, 22, 27
Catholic  34, 59
**Chalmers Close  46**, 47
**Characters at Home in the High Street**  30
*Checkmate*  12, 13, 20, 29, 49
**Church of the Trinity, The**  9, **46**–48, 51, 58, 71, 72
Clémence (of Coulanges)  10, 48, 54
Closes  11
Cochrane. *See* Tam Cochrane
**Conn's Close**  31, 41, **42**, 43
Constable's Tower: Edinburgh Castle  7, 14–16
Corstorphine  4
Covenanters  21, 24
**Covenanters' Memorial, The**  21
Cowgate Port  9, 50
**Cowgate, The**  2, 9, 12, 20, 21, **23**, 24, 26, 31, 32, 37, 42, 46, 50
**Craigmillar Castle**  3, **60**, 61, 63, 84
crames. *See* kraimes
Crawford family (in the House of Niccolo)  65
Crown Matrimonial, The  20
Crown of Scotland, The  20, 49
**Crown Square: Edinburgh Castle**  15, **18**, 20
Culters' house, The  11, 43, 44, 55

## D

Darnley Jewel, The  58
David de Salmeton (David Simpson)  46, 65
David I of Scotland  5, 6, 15
David II of Scotland  7, 17
David's Tower: Edinburgh Castle  7–9, 14–19, 60
*Disorderly Knights, The*  2, 3, 12, 23, 27, 30, 34, 36, 39, 40, 42, 43, 50, 72

79

Dominicans. *See* Blackfriars Monastery
Dow Craig. *See* Calton Hill
Duke of Burgundy's bath, The  16
**Dunbar's Close**  52, **55**
Dunedin  2, 3, 5

**E**

**Edinburgh Castle**  2–5, 7–10, 12, **14**–22, 26, 27, 30, 35, 56, 59, 60, 63
Edward Bonkle, Provost of the Church of the Trinity  48, 72
Edward II of England  6
Entry of Margaret of Denmark, The  51
Esplanade, Edinburgh Castle  2, 14, 15, 21, 24, 25

**F**

Fife  4, 5, 37
**Fight at the Altar, The**  **34**
Firth of Forth, The. *See* River Forth
**Flodden Wall, The**  9, 10, **21**–24, **50**, 52
Floory Land. *See* Ca' Niccolò
font: St Giles' Cathedral  33, 34
Foogs Gate: Edinburgh Castle  15
football  14–17
**football pitch, The**  15, 16
**Forewall Battery: Edinburgh Castle**  15, **16**
Franciscans. *See* Greyfriars
Francis Crawford of Lymond. *See* Lymond (Francis Crawford of Lymond)

**G**

Gabriel (Graham Reid Malett)  2, 33–37, 41, 45, 50
*Game of Kings, The*  1, 9, 10, 14, 17, 18, 21, 24, 25, 26, 27, 28, 29, 39, 42, 44, 45, 49, 58, 66, 67, 71, 72
Gelis (van Borselen)  13, 30, 38, 50, 53, 62, 64
*Gemini*  1, 3, 6, 12, 18, 19, 23, 26, 27, 29, 30, 32, 33, 35, 37–39, 43, 44, 46, 48, 51, 53, 54, 56, 60, 61, 64, 65, 67–70, 72
George Douglas, Sir  24, 27
George IV Bridge  2, 21, 22, 24, 25, 29, 31

George Paris  27, 40
**Gladstone's Land**  25, **28**, 39
golf  66
Gosford Close. *See* Mungo Tennant's House
**Granny's Green Steps**  21
**Grassmarket, The**  2, 9, 12, **20**–22, 24, 27, 45, 50, 71
Great Hall, Craigmillar Castle  62
**Great Hall: Edinburgh Castle**  15, 18, 19, **20**
Greenside  4, 44
Gregorio (of Asti)  51
Greyfriars Kirkyard  24
**Greyfriars Monastery**  9, 21, **24**

**H**

**Half Moon Battery: Edinburgh Castle**  14–**17**
**Halkerston's Wynd**  43, **46**
Heart of Midlothian, The  38
Henry de St Pol  20, 63
Hertford, Lord. *See* Somerset (Edward Seymour, Earl of Hertford and Duke of Somerset)
high altar: St Giles' Cathedral  6, 32–36
**High Kirk of St Giles, The.** *See* St Giles' Cathedral
**High Street, The**  2, 5, 8–12, 23, 26, 27, 29, **30**, 31, 33, 37, 39–47, 49–52, 54, 71
**Holyrood**  2, 3, 6–8, 11, 19, 50, 53, 55, **56**, 58, 59, 64, 65, 67, 71
Holyrood Abbey. *See* Abbey (Holyrood)
Holyrood Palace. *See* Palace of Holyroodhouse, The
Horse Market. *See* Grassmarket, The
House of Niccolò, The  1, 14, 45, 50
**Hub, The**  **27**, 28
Hugo vander Goes  48, 72

**J**

James I of Scotland  19
James II of Scotland  8, 16, 20, 47, 58
James III of Scotland  6, 10, 18, 19, 20, 24, 35, 58, 65, 73
James IV of Scotland  6, 7, 8, 20, 57
James V of Scotland  19, 49, 57, 58
James VI of Scotland  19, 28

James Liddell  19, 23
James Sandilands, Sir  23
**Jeffrey Street**  49, **51**, 52
Jerott Blyth  13, 23, 33, 34, 35, 36, 41
John Bonkle  48, 72
John (Johndie) Stewart, Earl of Mar  19, 54, 61, 63
John Knox  38, 44, 47, 48, 49
**John Knox House**  39, 47, **48**, 49
John, Master of Maxwell  58
Johnston Terrace  24, 26, 27
Jordan (de St Pol) de Ribérac  23, 30
jousting tournaments (*UH*)  20, 22, 24
Julius (of Bologna)  23, 43, 45, 51, 53, 64

**K**

Kathi (Kateljne Sersanders)  17, 22, 23, 30, 37, 39, 52, 53, 54, 65, 66
**Kathi and Robin's House**  52, **53**
Kerr family, The  41
**Kilmirren House**  12, 22, 23, 25, **26**, 30, 43, 45
*King Hereafter*  2, 3, 5, 16, 67
King's Wall, The  8, 9, 10, 22, 25
**King's Wark, The  65**
Kirkbraehead  4, 45
Kirk o' Field  9
Kirk o' Field Port. *See* Potterow Port
kraimes  39, 78

**L**

Lady Stair's Close. *See* Makars' Court
Lady Steps  33, 36, 37, 41
**Lamb's House  65**
lands  10, 11, 28, 45, 55, 78
**Lang Stairs: Edinburgh Castle  14**, 15, 16
Lauder's chapel: St Giles' Cathedral  37
**Lawnmarket**  2, 12, 21, 22, **24**–28, 45, 71
**Leith**  3, 4, 5, 7, 19, 46, 49, 51, 53, 55, 60, **63**–67
Leith History  63
**Leith Links  66**
Leith Strand  66
**Leith Wynd**  47, 50, **51**, 52, 53, 64
Liddell. *See* James Liddell
Lord Grey (Sir William Grey, 13th Baron Grey de Wilton)  27, 72
Lothian  2, 3, 5
luckenbooths  12, 28, 49
Luckenbooths  31, 32, 38, 39, 40, 41, 78
**Lymond and Leith  66**
Lymond Chronicles, The  1, 9, 14, 19, 50
Lymond (Francis Crawford of Lymond)  1–3, 9, 10, 12–14, 17–19, 21, 23, 24, 26–29, 34–37, 39, 41, 42, 44, 48, 49, 50, 55, 57, 58, 66, 72

**M**

Mad Martha  16
**Maison Dieu**  41, **42**, 43
**Makars' Court**  25, **28**, 29
Margaret Douglas, Countess of Lennox  58
Margaret of Denmark, Queen of James III of Scotland  22, 51, 58, 73
Margaret (St Margaret), mother of David I of Scotland  7, 15, 16, 58
Mary de Guise, Queen of James V of Scotland  19, 25, 26, 35, 71, 73
**Mary de Guise's Palace  25**, 26, 71
**Mary King's Close**  43, 44, **45**
Mary of Guelders, Queen of James II of Scotland  47, 58
Mary, Queen of Scots  7, 8, 16, 19, 24, 49, 55, 57, 58, 71–73
**Mercat Cross, The  42**
**Mons Meg: Edinburgh Castle**  15, **16**
Mossman family  19, 49
**Moubray House**  48, 49
Moultrie's Hill  4, 44, 46
Mound, The  2, 43
Mungo Tennant  10, 25, 28, 29, 72
**Mungo Tennant's House**  25, **29**
**Museum of Edinburgh, The  52**, 54
**Musselburgh**. *See* **Battle of Pinkie**

**N**

**National Gallery of Scotland, The**  2, 3, **72**
**National Library of Scotland, The**  3, **73**, 84
**National Museum of Scotland, The**  3, 24, 25, **71**
**Nativity Play, The**  3, 48, 56, **59**
**Netherbow Port, The**  47, **49**, 50

81

# Index

**Newbygging** 21
New Port 9, 46
**Nicholas and Leith** 64
**Nicholas's House** 25, **26**
Nicholas (vander Poele/de Fleury) 1, 2, 4, 11, 17, 19, 20, 22, 25, 26, 29, 30, 31, 38, 43, 45, 46, 48–51, 53, 54, 56, 59–64, 67–70
Nor' Loch, The 2, 4, 9, 10, 25, 29, 30, 44–46, 47, 49
**North Bridge** 2, 43, 44, **46**, 47
north door: St Giles' Cathedral 6, 33, 35

## O

octagonal pillars: St Giles' Cathedral 6, 36
Old Tolbooth, The. See Tolbooth, The (Edinburgh)
Old Town, The 2, 12, 25, 55
Osep Nepeja, Ambassador from Ivan IV of Muscovy 3, 4, 11

## P

**Palace of Holyroodhouse, The** 2, 7, 12, 19, 56, **57**, 58
**Palace Yard: Edinburgh Castle** 15, 16, 18
Parliament Hall 37
**Parliament Square** 31, 33, **37**
Pentland Hills 3, 4, 60, 64
Phemie (Euphemia) Dunbar 68, 70
physic garden. See Church of the Trinity, The
**Portcullis Gate: Edinburgh Castle** **14**, 15
Potterow Port 9
Preston Aisle: St Giles' Cathedral 32, 33
Preston family 6, 32, 33, 60
Princes Street/Princes Street Gardens 2, 11, 12, 44, 45
**Prisons of War: Edinburgh Castle** 15, 18, **20**
Protestant 8, 24, 34, 48

## R

Randy Bell 33, 36
Reformation, The 5, 6, 24, 32, 34, 37, 41, 49, 58, 73
relic/ reliquary 6, 7, 32, 34, 35

Richard Crawford, Third Baron Culter 25, 37, 66
**Riddles Court** 25, **28**
*Ringed Castle, The* 2, 4, 11
River Forth 4, 63
River Leith. *See* Water of Leith, The
Robert I (the Bruce) of Scotland 5
Robert II of Scotland 38
Robin (of Berecrofts) 17, 52, 53, 54
Roslin Castle. *See* Rosslyn Castle
**Roslin Village** 32, **68**
**Rosslyn Castle** **70**
Rosslyn Chapel 3, **68**, 84
Rough Wooing, The 7, 58, 67
Royal Gunhouse: Edinburgh Castle 19
Royal Mile, The 2, 10, 11, 20, 24, 27, 49, 78
**Royal Palace: Edinburgh Castle** 15, 18, **19**

## S

sacristy: Rosslyn Chapel 69
Salisbury Crags 3
Salt Tron, The 40, 43
Sandy. *See* Albany (Alexander 'Sandy' Stewart, Duke of Albany)
Sang School, The 37
Saunders. *See* Anselm Sersanders
*Scales of Gold* 71
**Scottish National Portrait Gallery, The** 3, **73**
Semple Close 26
Silvermills 4, 45
Sinclair (St Clair) family 32, 67, 68, 70
sluices 10, 46
Solway Moss 49, 58
Somerset (Edward Seymour, Earl of Hertford and Duke of Somerset) 7, 58, 66
South Bridge 2, 31
south door: St Giles' Cathedral 34
St Clair. *See* Sinclair (St Clair) family
St Giles 5, 6, 32, 34
**St Giles' Cathedral** 3, 5, 6, 24, 30, **31**–37, 38, 39, 41, 42, 44, 45, 72, 73, 78, 84
**St Giles' Kirkyard** 24, 31, **37**, 38, 78
Stinkand Raw, The. *See* Luckenbooths
Stinkand Style, The 32, 39, 41
**St John's Street and Cross** 54
St Margaret. *See* Margaret (St Margaret),

mother of David I of Scotland
**St Margaret's Chapel: Edinburgh Castle** 7, 15
St Mary's Port 9, 50
**St Mary's Street** 49, **50**, 52
**St Mary's Wynd 50**, 52, 53
St Pol house (mansion). *See* Kilmirren House
Sybilla, Dowager Lady Culter 26, 44–46, 51, 55
Sybilla's house. *See* Culters' house, The

**T**

Tam Cochrane 69
Telfer Wall, The 9, 10, 21
Thistle Chapel: St Giles' Cathedral 32, 33
Thomas Palmer, Sir 18
Thorfinn (Earl of Orkney and King of Alba) 2, 3, 5, 67
*To Lie With Lions* 1, 3, 5, 10, 13, 14, 16, 17, 18, 30, 31, 46, 48, 50, 53, 59, 64, 67, 72
Tobie (Tobias Beventini of Grado) 32, 52–54, 61, 63
**Tobie's House** 52, **53**, 63
**Tolbooth, The** (Edinburgh) 18, 31, 37, **38**, 39, 41, 78
**Tournament Grounds, The** 18, 21, **22**, 23, 27
Tournament of the Unicorn 22, 26
Trinity Altarpiece, The 72, 73
**Trinity Apse.** *See* Church of the Trinity, The
Trinity Church, The. *See* Church of the Trinity, The
**Tron Kirk** 31, **43**, 46

**U**

*Unicorn Hunt, The* 1, 20, 22, 23, 24, 26, 45, 51, 53, 58, 63, 64, 65, 66
**Upper Bow** (modern street) 21, 22, 24, 25, **27**
Upper (West) Bow (city gate) 9, 10, 21, 23

**V**

Vaults: Edinburgh Castle. *See* Prisons of War: Edinburgh Castle
**Vennel, The 21**, 78
Victoria Street 22, 23, 25

**W**

**Walls** 8
Walter (Wat) Scott of Buccleuch. *See* Buccleuch
Walter Scott, Sir 28, 38, 40
Wardrop's Court. *See* Makars' Court
**Warriston's Close** 43, **44**, 49
**Water Fountain** 47, **49**
Water of Leith, The 4, 63–65
**Water of Leith Walkway, The 65**
Waverley Station 2, 10, 47
**West Bow** (Street) 21, **22**, 23, 25–27, 40, 41, 45
**West Port** 9, **21**, 22
William Preston, Sir. *See* Preston family
Will Roger 33, 46, 48, 69, 70
Will Scott (Sir William Scott of Kincurd, Younger of Buccleuch) 18, 42, 49
Writers' Court. *See* Warriston's Close
**Writers' Museum, The** 25, **28**, 29

## Publishing Information

Published by the Dorothy Dunnett Society,
Edinburgh, Scotland
Scottish Charity No. SC030649
www.dorothydunnett.org

Copyright © The Dorothy Dunnett Society 2015
Photographs © the individual photographers

First published by the Dorothy Dunnett Society in 2015

Text and Maps: Nicky Cannon
Series Editor: Jenny Myers
Editor and Design: Suzanne McNeill

Nicky Cannon has asserted her right under the Copyright, Designs and Patents Act 1988 to be identified as the author of this work.

All rights reserved. Apart from any fair dealing for the purpose of private study, research, criticism or review, as permitted under the Copyright, Designs and Patents Act 1988, no part of this publication may be reproduced, stored in a retrieval system, or transmitted in any form or by any means, electronic, mechanical, photocopying, recording or otherwise, without the prior written permission of the copyright owner.

Every attempt has been made by the publisher to secure the appropriate permissions for material reproduced in this book. If there has been an oversight we will be happy to rectify the situation. Written submission should be made to the publishers.

ISBN: 978-0-9570046-3-4

Printed and bound by Printwell Limited,
3 Callon Street, Airdrie, ML6 6BW, Scotland.

## Acknowledgements

Many sources and friends have helped in preparing this text. The author wishes especially to thank all concerned at the Dorothy Dunnett Society, Rosalind Marshall for helping iron out details regarding St Giles', Alan Cannon for technical help, Amelia Cannon for accompanying the author on site visits, and both Alan and Amelia for their support.

The Dorothy Dunnett Society also thanks Penguin Books for permitting us to reproduce the quotations from the novels.

## Photographic and Illustration Credits

The Dorothy Dunnett Society particularly wishes to thank the National Library of Scotland (NLS) for permission to reproduce the historical maps of Scotland published in this guide, Peter Stubbs of www.edinphoto.org.uk for allowing us to reproduce the engravings of old Edinburgh from his website, and Vic Sharp Photography 2015 of www.mistyriver.co.uk for giving us permission to reproduce his photograph of the interior of Rosslyn Chapel.

Front cover: Nicky Cannon (Craigmillar Castle); NLS (G. Braun & F. Hogenberg, 'Edenburgum, Scotiae Metropolis, 1582').
Back cover: Colin McMillan (roses on Makars' Court stone); Anne Buchanan (Abbey ruins)
Text pages: Amelia Cannon (68)
Anne Buchanan (8)
Battlefields Trust, www.battlefieldstrust.com, G Foard (66)
Colin McMillan (29)
Derick Monaghan (6, 17, 19)
National Library of Israel (64)
National Library of Scotland (1, 23, 74–77)
Nicky Cannon (32, 42, 55, 56, 57)
Peter Stubbs, www.edinphoto.org.uk (11, 27, 38, 50)
© Courtesy of RCAHMS (35, 40, 47, 48) Licensor www.rcahms.gov.uk
Tom Blackie (title page)
© Vic Sharp Photography 2015, www.mistyriver.co.uk (69)